FOOTPRINTS IN THE SAND:
Brecknock Notabilities

FOOTPRINTS IN THE SAND:
Brecknock Notabilities

W.S.K. Thomas

First impression—October 1994

ISBN 1 85902 143 3

Printed by J.D. Lewis and Sons Ltd., Gomer Press, Llandysul, Dyfed.

I
Rebecca
wyres i fi

Contents

	page
Foreword	ix
Preface	x
Illustrations	xiii
Maps	xiii
Introduction	xiv
1. Gerald of Wales	1
2. Dafydd Gam	13
3. Sir John Price	20
4. John Penry	34
5. Colonel Jenkin Jones	56
6. Howell Harris	65
7. Dr Thomas Coke	86
8. Sarah Siddons	99
9. Theophilus Jones	115
10. Adelina Patti	125
Bibliography	147
Index	149

Foreword

One of the most rewarding things about being a university teacher is that you can become such good friends with your students. Dr W.S.K. Thomas is one of those who has remained among my closest friends since his college days. What has brought us particularly near to one another in recent years has been his continuing interest in writing history. Those who know Brecon at all will be keenly aware of the attractiveness of the ancient borough and its charming environs. They will hardly be surprised that an accomplished historian like Dr Thomas, who has for over thirty years made his home in the town, should be deeply drawn to its history. He has already given us a delightful history of Brecon from 1093 to 1660 and another absorbing volume on the town in Georgian and Victorian times. He now presents the third part of his trilogy —Notabilities of Brecon. He has made a varied and attractive selection of ten of the outstanding characters who were born in or near Brecon, or else became intimately associated with it. Each of the ten is a striking personality in his or her own right, and all have contributed richly to the long and colourful tapestry of Brecon life from the middle ages to recent days. Their stories have been told in vivid, concise and readable fashion, which I feel sure that the reader will enjoy as greatly as I did. I congratulate the author heartily on his achievement and commend his book most warmly to the public, both inside and outside Brecon.

Glanmor Williams

Preface

This is the third volume of a trilogy on the history of Brecknock. Many local historians have laboured in this vineyard, and my debt to them will be apparent and is readily acknowledged. I can only trust that they will accept this present volume as a token of my appreciation and gratitude.

Throughout the time that I was engaged in researching and writing the book, ready encouragement and sound advice were always forthcoming from a scholar who has guided my footsteps since undergraduate days. Professor Glanmor Williams read the whole book in typescript, and his perceptive comments not only enabled me to avoid some of the many pitfalls that were liberally strewn along the way, but they also greatly enriched and enlivened the volume. My debt to him is incalculable. Needless to say, for any errors of omission or commission that still remain, I hold myself entirely responsible.

Colleagues of mine at Brecon High School have also been ready with their support, and I wish to thank three in particular, Mr Stanley Foulkes, Mrs Eira Jones and Dr W. Ll. Williams. Mr Foulkes and Mrs Jones proof read the galley sheets with meticulous care, and I am extremely grateful to them for their painstaking efforts. Dr Williams, who is no mean cartographer despite the fact that he is a biologist by inclination and training, undertook the task of preparing the local maps and I am very appreciative of his skill. Finally, I wish to thank Mr Glanville Francis Thomas, like myself a happily retired headteacher, for the considerable interest which he took in the production of this volume from conception to birth.

The staff of Brecon Library are also deserving of my gratitude since they spared no effort in procuring for me the essential bricks without which this book could never have been constructed. In this context I wish to thank in particular Mr Christopher Price, Deputy Area Librarian, for his understanding and tolerance despite the constant and heavy demands which I made upon both these qualities. It is also a pleasure to express one's gratitude to Dr Dyfed Elis-Gruffydd of Gomer Press for his unfailing courtesy when guiding the book through the various stages of publication.

Finally, I wish to thank my wife and family for their unwavering support and encouragement at all times. There were occasions when they must have felt that I was spending the greater part of my time in the past, and it was a considerable relief to them when, occasionally, I surfaced in the present. Yet, my sojourns in bygone ages were borne with patience and fortitude, even those golden moments I spent in the company of Sarah and Adelina. I can only hope that the volume will help to compensate for those long hours spent in entertaining so many of Brecknock's past notabilities under the family roof.

Illustrations

	page
Manorbier Castle: Gerald's birthplace	2
Gerald's home at Llanddew: a Gothic doorway	4
Gerald's statue	11
The battle of Agincourt from a fifteenth-century French miniature	16
Newton: an ancestral home of the Games' family	18
Priory House: as it is today	24
Yny Lhyvyr Hwnn: frontispiece	26
Cefn Brith, Llangamarch, birthplace of John Penry	36
The Aequity: John Penry's first book	39
Printing press of the kind used by John Penry	44
Llanddeti Church	57
The door at Llanddeti at which Jenkin Jones discharged his pistol	62
Trefeca	79
Trefeca College	81
Howell Harris	84
Thomas Coke	95
Birthplace of Thomas Coke	95
The Dr Coke Memorial Schools	97
Sarah Siddons as Mrs Haller	100
Birthplace of Sarah Siddons	104
Theophilus Jones's house in Lion Street	118
Theophilus Jones: a drawing by Thomas Price	122
Adelina Patti	126
Ernesto Nicolini	134
Casket presented to Adelina containing the freedom of Brecon	138
Craig-y-nos Castle	141

Maps

	page
Gerald's itinerary through Wales	7
France in the early fifteenth century	17
Breconshire's Methodist connections	70

xiii

Introduction

Great historical events and trends are not chronicled in this volume. This is a book about people. They were not ordinary people, but people possessed of exceptional talents, who left an imprint in the sands of time. Personalities in the present age loom large. They figure prominently in cinemas, newspapers, magazines and on television, and by these means they are introduced into the privacy of our homes and become *foci* of attention and debate. But this preoccupation with royalty, politicians, film stars, footballers, and athletes has meant that the famous figures of the past are becoming largely forgotten. They are buried under a mass of human débris. Most people in Brecknock will have heard of Barry John, but how many will have heard about Sir John Price? If Howell Harris and Adelina Patti were suddenly to appear in the streets of the ancient borough of Brecon, how many of its worthy citizens would recognise them, let alone know anything at all about them? In a way this is an attempt to breathe new life into old bones, and revive interest in people who, in one way or another, contributed a great deal to the fabric of life in days long gone by.

Considering that the field is so wide and varied, it is a very invidious task to decide which ten lives deserve special attention. The situation can be likened to selecting a winner when there is a blanket finish to a race. The final choice is bound to reflect one's own personal predilections, but given this inevitable limitation, I have tried to make my list as broadly based as possible to reflect the many facets of life in Brecknockshire through the centuries. Thus Dafydd Gam and Colonel Jenkin Jones are the swordsmen, the men of action, while the *literati* are represented by scribes of the calibre of Sir John Price and Theophilus Jones. Clerics, as befits a cathedral town, have their niche, and in their ranks were worthies of considerable stature, people like Giraldus Cambrensis, John Penry, Thomas Coke and Howell Harris. And finally the ranks of Brecknock thespians and singers were exalted by the presence of colossi like Sarah Siddons and Adelina Patti, Sarah as possibly the best tragedienne ever to have graced the boards, and Adelina as arguably the greatest diva of all times.

This book of great lives is for the general reader; though, hopefully, the professional historian may find something of value in it. The volume presents the human face of local history, and I trust that its appeal will transcend the boundaries of Brecknock, for the personalities dealt with are of more than local or passing interest. Indeed, some bestrode whole continents, and their achievements are still visible today. Much is owed by Welsh Calvinistic Methodism to the organising genius of Howell Harris, while Thomas Coke was the founder of the Wesleyan episcopal church in America; Sir John Price was responsible for the first Welsh printed book, while Theophilus Jones's herculean labours resulted in the production of the finest of the Welsh county histories. These are no mean achievements and Brecknock should be proud that her soil should have nurtured individuals of such excellence.

Though this is a collection of short biographies, not all of those whose lives are recounted were natives of the area. Giraldus Cambrensis was born in Pembroke though, as archdeacon of Brecon, he was to live in Llanddew, a residence for which he displayed a particular fondness; Sarah Siddons first saw the light of day in the 'Shoulder of Mutton' because her mother's travelling company happened to be performing in Brecon at the time; Adelina Patti uttered her first trill in Madrid, and though she became an international celebrity, she chose to live in a chateau situated in the upper reaches of the Swansea valley. Adelina, as an Italian, was a rank outsider, and some vestiges of the splendour which characterised her reign at Craig-y-nos still cling to that once magnificent, though now somewhat decayed, pile.

In presenting these ten Brecknock snapshots, I decided to embrace the chronological approach because it appeared to me to possess the cardinal virtue of being singularly uncomplicated. I can only hope that the reader will endorse my judgement both with regard to the personalities paraded and the procedure adopted.

Lives of great men all remind us
We can make our lives sublime,
And, departing, leave behind us
Footprints on the sands of time.

Henry Wadsworth Longfellow (1807-1882)

GERALD THE WELSHMAN
GIRALDUS CAMBRENSIS *c.* 1146-1223

I was sprung from the princes of Wales and from the barons
of the Marches, and when I see injustice in either race I hate
it.

So exclaimed Gerald proudly about his lineage. He was born *c.*
1146, and spent his boyhood at Manorbier castle, near Tenby in
Pembrokeshire. He was the youngest son of William de Barri[1]
and Angharad, the daughter of Gerald de Windsor and his wife
Nest. Nest was a Welsh princess and reputedly the most beautiful
woman in Wales.[2] She was the daughter of Rhys ap Tewdwr, the
King of Deheubarth, who died fighting the Normans at Battle, a
few miles to the north-west of Brecon, in 1093. Gerald was,
therefore, a man of mixed birth and he gloried in it. In his veins
ran the blood of Welsh princes and Norman barons, which led
him to remark bitterly on one occasion that 'both groups
regarded him as a stranger'. But despite his ready sympathy for
the Welsh and admiration for their virtues—he had a smattering
of their tongue[3]—his ultimate loyalty was always to remain with
his Anglo-Norman kinfolk.

His uncle David Fitzgerald, the bishop of St David's, the oldest
and most important diocese in Wales, assumed responsibility for
Gerald's early education and he arranged for two clerics to
instruct him. As a younger son, from an early age he was destined
for holy orders, and as a boy he used to build churches in the sand
on the seashore at Manorbier. But his first steps in education were
tentative and painful, and it took the chidings of his uncle and the
taunts of his tutors to goad him into greater effort. When
sufficient progress had been made he was sent to the great abbey
of St Peter in Gloucester, where his tutor was master Homo, a
renowned teacher and scholar. However, this was an age when
young men with Gerald's background travelled far and wide to
study at centres of excellence, and Gerald became a student at the
University of Paris, where he completed the seven year course in
the liberal arts, embracing grammar, logic and rhetoric. It was at

Manorbier Castle: Gerald's birthplace
Courtesy of Robina Elis-Gruffydd

Paris, also, that he gained a mastery of canon law. According to Gerald, who always had a good conceit of his own abilities, during the time which he spent there he created such a favourable impression that, when the tutors were asked for an example of the perfect student, his was the name that first came to mind.

In 1174, when he was twenty-eight years of age, he left Paris and on his return to Wales he was appointed to a plurality of livings through the influence which Bishop David, his father's brother, and his friends, were able to exercise. Pluralism was practised very widely in the Middle Ages, especially among the higher clergy. Gerald, in addition to his ecclesiastical offices at Hereford and Mathry, became vicar of parishes as disparate as Angle, Tenby, Llanwnda, Laugharne and Chesterton. He was never resident in any of them and the result, inevitably, was a general neglect of pastoral duties since the work was delegated to poorly educated and badly paid curates. Gerald, who could be very critical of what he regarded as deficiencies in the church—he was an offspring of the reform movement which was sweeping through the church and had drunk deeply of the pure milk of its doctrine that the church should be freed from lay control—never saw the mote in his own eye. He now went to Canterbury and received a commission from Richard, the Archbishop who, on 7 April, had been appointed Papal Legate, to enforce the payment of tithes on wool and cheese in the diocese of St David's. However, owing to royal interference, the Flemings in Pembroke were exempted, much to the annoyance of the local Welsh, who also wished to be relieved of the impost. Gerald now demonstrated that he was a person of strong determination and unflagging energy—he even disciplined the sheriff of Pembroke, William Carquit—traits which earned him the enmity of many of the Normans and Flemings in the diocese. Indeed one knight, Richard fitz Tancred, even threatened him with death.

While at Brecknock to execute the Archbishop's injunction, Gerald discovered that the archdeacon,[4] an elderly man by the name of Jordan, publicly kept a concubine at his home, conduct which ran contrary to canon law, which required priests to be celibate. Gerald now commanded the archdeacon, who had been in trouble with the church on several previous occasions, to set the woman aside. This he not only refused to do but in the process also roundly vilified Gerald and the Archbishop. The office of archdeacon was now conferred on Gerald, but he was always to remain a little sensitive about the manner in which he had obtained it. His new found authority enabled Gerald to travel around the archdeaconry, and he tackled fearlessly many of the abuses in clerical practices which he encountered. He returned finally to his house at Llanddew, to which he was very attached and where he entertained Archbishop Baldwin in 1188.

In 1176 David Fitzgerald died and Gerald was the favoured candidate of the cathedral chapter to succeed him as bishop. Henry II, however, refused to recognise his nomination by the canons because of the irregularity of the proceedings and his kinship with the princes and great men of Wales. Instead, he enforced the election of Peter of Lee, the Cluniac prior of Wenlock. His disappointment at this rejection led Gerald to return to his books, and the years 1177-79 were again spent at the

University of Paris where, according to his own testimony, he became a very successful lecturer. It has to be said that a becoming modesty was not one of Gerald's virtues.

For whatever reason, Gerald now returned to England, arriving at Canterbury on Trinity Sunday, 1179. By this time Peter of Lee had been driven from Wales on account of a dispute between himself and the Welsh. He now committed the care and custody of his bishopric to Gerald. The two made uneasy bedfellows and when the bishop, without consulting his colleague, suspended some of the canons and archdeacons of St David's, and excommunicated others, Gerald resigned his custody of the see and threw in his lot with the chapter.

Tiring of these tedious quarrels Gerald, in 1183, in the capacity of an observer, visited Ireland with his eldest brother, Philip. On his return he was summoned to court by Henry II, who was then in the Marches working for the pacification of Wales. He needed Gerald's services as a mediator between the court and Rhys ap

Gerald's home at Llanddew: a Gothic doorway

Gruffydd, the lord of Deheubarth, known in history as 'Yr Arglwydd Rhys' (The Lord Rhys). Rhys wished to recover lands which had been lost as a result of the Norman incursions. After initial setbacks, he had taken advantage of Henry's problems in England to re-establish his hegemony in Deheubarth, a pre-eminence he was able to maintain until the time of this death in 1197.

In 1185, possibly on account of the closeness of his relationship with the conquerors of Ireland, for amongst these *conquistadores* were his mother's brothers and half-brothers, he was appointed to accompany Prince John to the Emerald Isle. The party took ship at Milford Haven on 25 April and landed at Waterford the next day. He was now offered, and refused, the two Irish bishoprics of Wexford and Leighlin. This second visit, which lasted a year, he turned to good account by continuing to collect materials for two volumes on the history and geography of Ireland: the *Expugnatio Hibernica* and the *Topographia Hibernica*. It was at his palace at Llanddew that these books were completed, but it was at Oxford, one of the greatest seats of learning in England, that he introduced and sought to publicise them to the outside world.

But his perambulations were not over yet, and in March 1188 he accompanied Archbishop Baldwin on his celebrated tour through Wales for the purpose of drumming up support for the Third Crusade in which Henry's own son, Richard, the future Richard I, was to become personally involved. The mission was an official one, since the Archbishop was dispatched to Wales by the King. Henry II's motives were more political than religious, for he wished to divert Welsh energies into fighting the infidel rather than the English. Whilst Baldwin's sincerity for the Crusade can never be questioned—he gave his life for it—the itinerary did, nevertheless, provide him with the opportunity of asserting his metropolitan authority over the Welsh dioceses. This was demonstrated when he celebrated mass at the high altars of Llandaff, St David's, Bangor and St Asaph. As with Ireland, Gerald found it irresistible to put pen to paper, and an account of this journey through Wales is contained in his *Itinerarium*

Kambriae (Itinerary through Wales) which first appeared in 1191.[5]

The itinerary started at Hereford, and the company followed the coastal road around south, west and north Wales before finally returning to the starting point at Hereford. The perambulation took five weeks or so to accomplish and, according to Gerald, about 3,000 men were prevailed upon to volunteer their services to help in freeing Palestine from the infidel Turk. However, it has to be said that though some 3,000 men had been prevailed upon, in the heat of the moment, to offer their blades, not all would have actually gone on crusade. At New Radnor, following a fiery sermon by Archbishop Baldwin, Gerald himself had been the first to step forward to take the vow, though he was destined never to fight in the Holy land.[6] Many were freed from their oaths by promising to contribute financially towards the cost of the Crusade and by giving assurances that they would strive to improve the condition of the church in their own localities.

Gerald, who had a particular fondness for tales with miraculous overtones, mentions three such stories appertaining to Brecon. One related to the singing birds of Llangorse Lake, and how its waters would change colour from green to red. Another referred to the chapel of St Eluned situated on an eminence about a mile to the east of the town. Eluned, the twenty-third of Brychan's twenty-four saintly daughters, was martyred at Slwch defending her chastity. Thereafter, annually, on 1 August, the sick would resort to her shrine from far and wide and, after indulging in frenzied religious dances in the churchyard, would be led with their oblations to the altar where many would be cured of their afflictions. Finally, he recounts how a boy, in the act of removing some young pigeons from their nest inside the church of St David in Llanfaes, had his hand immovably fixed to the stone on which he had been leaning. It took three days and nights of prayer and supplication for the hand to be released.

In 1194 Gerald produced another notable book on Wales, the *Description of Wales*, and while the *Itinerary* had been full of shrewd digressions relating to the topography, antiquities, polit-

GERALD'S ITINERARY THROUGH WALES, 1188

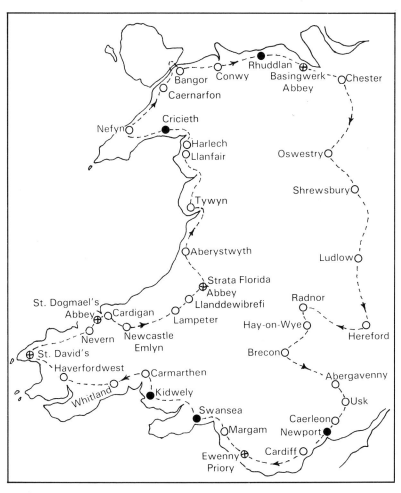

O Places visited

⊕ overnight stay at a religious house

● Overnight stay at a castle

0   25

Statute Miles

ics, religious rites, customs and superstitions of ordinary people, the *Description* was methodical and objective. Its four sections deal with the geography of Wales; the virtues of the Welsh; their vices—particularly their moral short-comings; how the Norman invaders could best conquer Wales, and how the Welsh could best resist them. His is not a complete picture of Wales, for he concentrated on those features which helped to distinguish the Welsh from their Anglo-Norman neighbours; he also underestimated the wide social and regional differences in the country; and his portrait is rather static and makes little reference to the profound changes taking place in the fabric of Welsh society.

On account of the disorders in France, early in 1189, Baldwin and Ranulph Glanvill, the Justiciar, left for France and Gerald accompanied them. However, the death of the King greatly disturbed Wales and Gerald was now sent by Richard I to preserve the peace there. Following Richard's coronation, there was one obstacle which had to be removed before Gerald could resume full royal employment. He had vowed at New Radnor to go on crusade,[7] and an absolution from that vow was now required. This he received from the cardinal legate, John of Agnani, on the grounds that his poverty would not allow him to go. He was now offered the bishoprics of Bangor and St Asaph; but he refused both, as his mind was set on occupying David's chair.

After 1193 Richard I left the administration of his kingdom in the capable hands of Hubert Walter, the Archbishop of Canterbury, a man greatly disliked by Gerald. But Gerald was getting increasingly bored with the monotony and dull inactivity of court life and so he decided to relinquish his office under the crown, and to resume his studies, especially of theology, a field in which he was particularly conscious of his deficiencies. After a stay in Hereford, he moved to Lincoln, which had the best school of theology in England, leaving his archdeaconry of Brecon in the care of a local cleric. He was not entirely devoid of influential friends at court since Prince John, whom he had accompanied to Ireland years earlier, still held him in favour. He had entertained hopes of returning to Paris to continue his study of theology, but the renewal of hostilities between Philip Augustus and Richard I in France precluded that possibility. And so he had to remain at Lincoln, where he spent the greater part of his remaining years.

But the period which was to bring him considerable renown, and an even greater degree of personal frustration, was about to dawn. On 16 July 1198 Peter of Lee, bishop of St David's, died and on 29 July 1199 the chapter elected Gerald as their new bishop from a short list of four archdeacons. Though Peter had been elected bishop in 1178, his stay in the diocese had been very brief, and he ended his days in Tewkesbury. Between 1179-83 Gerald had officiated in his place—he was bishop in all but name—and though some ill feeling had crept into the relationship between him and the bishop after that date, sufficient good will remained to enable them to embark on the building of a new cathedral church, which still stands today. In the 1190s the quarrel became more embittered and it was still simmering when Peter died. But there was more at stake here than the appointment of a new bishop, and that was why not one of the four candidates found favour with the King and Hubert Walter. The real issue was the recognition of St David's as a metropolitan see independent of Canterbury. The conflict lasted for five years, and Gerald conducted a vigorous propaganda campaign to achieve his ends. Though he had been elected by the canons, he had not been consecrated bishop because of the opposition from London and Canterbury, and the impasse could only be resolved by a direct appeal to the Pope himself at Rome. This Gerald now undertook, and he visited the Holy City on three separate occasions to fight his corner. He reminded the Pope that until the reign of Henry I (1100-1135) the Welsh church had been subject only to Rome. From Innocent 111, however, he received no joy despite Gerald's presentation to him of six of his books. Gerald failed to appreciate that it was his very suitability for the post—his Welshness, his aristocratic connections, his learning and his personal energy— which made him unsuitable in the eyes of his opponents. They were convinced that, as bishop of St David's, he would have presented serious problems. He continued to seek the help of the Welsh princes, and most were eventually persuaded to lend him their support. Among them was the youthful prince of Gwynedd,

Llywelyn ap Iorwerth, Llywelyn the Great, who declared that
Gerald's fight for St David's would be remembered 'as long as
Wales should stand'. It was not until 1920 that Gerald's dream of
an independent Welsh church was realised, though Owain
Glyndŵr had proposed the idea in 1406.

The final humiliation came in 1203. By then, even his supporters at St David's had deserted him and, in November, Geoffrey of
Henlaw, the prior of Llanthony, the Archbishop's physician, was
appointed bishop. Gerald now abandoned the uneven struggle,
and a settlement was thrashed out in the winter of 1203-4 with
Hubert Walter. By its terms Gerald accepted Geoffrey's appointment, promised never again to advance the claims of St David's
during the Archbishop's lifetime, and surrendered the office of
archdeacon of Brecon. At the Pope's direction the Archbishop
agreed to reimburse Gerald for the heavy debts he had incurred
over the years in pressing the claims of his beloved see.

Gerald now took a step which he was long to regret. He asked
the Archbishop to support the appointment of his nephew,
another Gerald de Barri, the youngest son of his eldest brother
Philip, as his successor in the office of archdeacon of Brecon. The
Archbishop hesitated but finally agreed.

The final years of a very eventful life were spent with his books
at Lincoln, though he did visit Ireland and embarked upon a
spiritual pilgrimage to Rome in 1205. There was talk that he was
offered a cardinal's hat. However, his peace was to be disturbed
by a rapid deterioration in his relationship with his nephew,[8] and
his tutor, William de Capella, who acquired the living of Llanhamlach, and this domestic drama revolved around the administration of the archdeaconry which had been left in Gerald's
hands. Further there is a suggestion in his writings that he might
have been involved in the barons' struggle against King John.
Abandoned by his erstwhile friends, with doors which had always
been open to him now closed, he died at Manorbier in March 1223
at the ripe old age of seventy-seven, a tired and disappointed
man. According to tradition he was, fittingly, buried at St
David's, for he had been a doughty champion of the ancient
rights and privileges of that see. In Trinity chapel, within the

Gerald's statue

cathedral, there stands a statue of him. Though the sculptor depicts him as a scholar, a mitre is placed at his feet signifying his failure to achieve his life's ambition.

Whatever his faults, and they were many—he was inordinately proud, quarrelsome, opinionated, conceited, sensitive to criticism and impatient of obstacles—it is still undeniable that he was the most learned of men, and possessed of one of the liveliest minds and swiftest pens of the Middle Ages. His books, written in Latin about things Welsh, are a veritable quarry of information about Wales and her people which historians, over the ages, have drawn upon unstintingly. Though he wrote of the present, he had an eye to the future, for he always felt that posterity would justify him. A champion of St David's he undoubtedly was, but he fought indomitably for a cause that was even greater, and that was Wales herself.

NOTES

[1] The de Barris had been in the vanguard of the Norman conquest of Glamorgan and the family had taken its name from the island of Barry. Gerald was the youngest of four sons.

[2] She was referred to as the 'Helen of Wales' and earned a certain notoriety for her marital infidelities.

[3] When Gerald accompanied Archbishop Baldwin in his itinerary around Wales, he preached at a number of centres, but he always preached in French or Latin. The inference is that his Welsh was not sufficiently good for formal purposes.

[4] Archdeacons have been described as 'the eyes and ears of the bishop'.

[5] The *Itinerary* is more in the nature of an autobiography than an account of a tour through Wales for the central figure is not the Archbishop but Gerald himself.

[6] Infra, p. 8

[7] Supra, p. 6

[8] The young Gerald's chief delights were hunting, strumming barbarous Welsh melodies upon the harp, playing with cats and dogs, and making faces at his uncle.

DAFYDD GAM (d. 1415)

Dafydd Gam, or Dafydd ap Llywelyn, a Welsh warrior of considerable renown, was the scion of a family which, in order to
promote its own interests, identified itself with the ruling dynasty
of the day. This, perhaps, was an attitude which did not endear it
to many of the local Welsh, who entertained feelings of deep anti-
pathy towards the English colonial settlers. Dafydd's father was
Llywelyn ap Hywel Fychan, a Brecknock landowner descended
from Einion Sais.[1]

Einion had fought under Edward III at Crecy (1346) and Poitiers (1356) and, after a lengthy residence in England, had returned
to Wales enriched by the spoils of war. He took as his wife the
wealthy heiress of Hywel, lord of Miskin in Glamorgan. Einion
now became a substantial landowner in his own right by purchasing the whole of what was later called the hundred of Defynnog,
from Llywel on the border of Carmarthenshire to the river Tarell
outside Brecon. He built as a home for himself a castellated
mansion near the fall of a small brook into the river Usk at Penpont, some four miles to the west of Brecon on the road leading to
Llandovery. It is quite possible that a fortress had been erected
there before the incursion of the Normans into Brecknock.
Nothing now remains of this stronghold though Hugh Thomas,
the Breconshire Herald, writing in 1698, recalls having seen the
ruins, and Theophilus Jones, the renowned local antiquary, avers
that there were people living in 1805 who remembered the
rubbish, and the stones from the walls, being removed.

Dafydd was born into a most uncertain world. Wales was
suffering from the effects of the Black Death 1349 and the subsequent plagues which had resulted in the population being
reduced by a third or even a half. There had followed in the wake
of this dramatic fall in the demographic curve an agricultural and
a trade depression, and since most people at that time were, in one
way or another, engaged in agricultural pursuits, with the
emphasis very much on pastoral farming, the extent of the hardship can readily be appreciated. Edward I's conquest of Wales in

1282-3 had effectively partitioned the country into two quite
distinct, and mutually exclusive, areas: on the one hand, located
mainly in the west, was the Principality, consisting of the six
shires of Anglesey, Caernarvon, Merioneth, Cardigan, Carmarthen and Flint; and on the other hand, situated to the east, were
the Marcher Lordships. In the Principality, where the English
system of law and administration had been introduced, there was
a certain degree of law and order, but in the Marches there was
nothing but 'prodigal anarchy', though the extent of the lawless-
ness has doubtless been grossly exaggerated by some historians.
Here, power lay in the hands of mighty marcher lords who had
their own fortresses, their own private armies, their own systems
of administration, their own coinage, and their own laws and law
courts. The penetration of English influences accelerated the
decay of native Welsh institutions and the dissolution of the trad-
itional fabric of Welsh society. The resultant dislocation created
resentment, and the discontent of the Welsh found expression in
periodic revolts like those of Llywelyn Bren (1316), Owain Lawgoch (1372) and, more importantly, Owain Glyndŵr (1400-15).

However, even in the midst of this chaos, there were some fortunate families that prospered, and Dafydd's was one of these.
From Einion Sais he had inherited substantial estates in the
vicinity of Brecon and Llywel, and this legacy had been greatly
augmented by his father, Llywelyn, who, for 300 marks, had
purchased the mansions and lands of Peyton—Peityn Gwyn,
Peityn Du and Peityn Glas—in the parishes of Garthbrengy and
Llanddew from William Peyton, the last of that Norman family
to reside in Brecknock.

Dafydd, in a fit of bucolic temper, was almost to throw all these
advantages away when he became involved in a fierce family
quarrel with Richard Fawr[2] of Slwch. In the High Street of
Brecon, then a small market town, and the administrative centre
and hub of the economic life of the seignory of Brecknock,
Dafydd, in a fit of passion, cut down his relative. For this grue-
some deed he was declared an outlaw and was constrained to flee
to England, where he placed himself under the protection of King
Henry IV (1399-1413). It was no chance that took him to the court

of the English monarch, since Henry was known to Dafydd in his capacity as lord of Brecknock, a status which he had acquired through his marriage to Mary of Bohun. Thereafter, Dafydd was to remain a loyal and staunch supporter of the Lancastrian dynasty.

It was in April 1400 that Dafydd made his first appearance in the official records as the King's esquire[3] for which he received the rather handsome remuneration of forty marks a year.[4] But his unswerving loyalty to the King was now to be demonstrated by his unceasing hostility to Owain Glyndŵr who, in September 1400, had raised rebellion at Rhuthun. The immediate cause of the revolt was a landed dispute between Owain and Reginald Grey, lord of Rhuthun. However, what started as a local uprising by a disgruntled Welsh marcher lord came to embrace the whole country, since Owain struck deep chords in the national consciousness, and his cause was further fomented by the general distress consequent upon the rapid changes taking place in Welsh society and the Welsh economy.

The government, in November 1401, in accordance with accepted practice, rewarded Dafydd for his untiring efforts against Glyndŵr, by conveying to him rebel lands. On 5 May 1405 he played a part in the royal victory over Owain at Pwll Melyn, near Usk. His presence at the battle makes highly improbable the story of his allegedly treacherous attempt to assassinate Glyndŵr at the parliament which the latter held at Machynlleth in 1404.[5] What is certain is that Dafydd did fall into the clutches of the Welsh leader, though his capture must have taken place at a much later date. It was only in June 1412, when the revolt was petering out, that the seneschal[6] and receiver of Brecon, with the assent of Llywelyn ap Hywel, Dafydd's father, entered into negotiations with Glyndŵr to secure the release of 'David Gamm, tenant in the lordship of Brecon'.[7] Success accompanied these talks and Dafydd, apparently after the payment of a ransom of 700 marks,[8] was freed. In the meantime Owain had destroyed Gam's paternal residence at Peytin Gwyn and, according to Hugh Thomas, 'presumably that of Einion Sais, which was never rebuilt'.

A condition of Dafydd's release was that he should not engage in any further actions against Glyndŵr. Dafydd, however, on his return to Brecknock, was soon in breach of his parole since he vigorously persecuted those who remained loyal to Glyndŵr. Indeed, he may well have been instrumental in securing the destruction of Edmund Mortimer's castle at Dinas in retaliation for the latter's close alliance with Glyndŵr, which had been cemented by Mortimer's marriage to Glyndŵr's daughter, Catherine. Leland, who undertook his celebrated 'Itinerary' of Henry VIII's Kingdom in the 1530s, was to remark that 'the people about Dinas did burne Dinas Castel that oene Glindour shuld not kepe it for his forteres.[9]

But the final act in the colourful life of this doughty warrior and semi-legendary figure was to be enacted not on his native heath, but on a foreign field. At Agincourt, now in the Pas-de-

The battle of Agincourt from a fifteenth-century French miniature

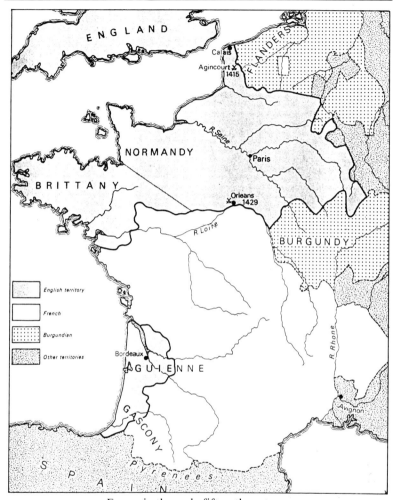

France in the early fifteenth century

Calais, on 25 October 1415, in one of the major battles of the Hundred Years' War between England and France, Dafydd was slain. Prior to the action, he had been sent to reconnoitre the enemy lines. On his return he is said to have reported to his youthful royal master, Henry V, concerned at his lack of numbers when compared with those of the French host, that 'there were men enough to be killed; men enough to be taken; and men enough to run away'. Before meeting his own end, Dafydd, in the heat of the battle, slew the Duke of Nevers with his own hand, and bore away his arms which, ever after, were to be used by his descendants. After the battle, when Henry was informed that Dafydd was on the point of death, he hurried to his side and, according to tradition, knighted him on that bloodstained field. [10]

Gam, Shakespeare's 'Fluellen' in Henry IV, may well, like Fluellen, have been 'good natured, brave, choleric and pedantic'. Certainly his exploits at home and abroad attested to his courage. That he had some physical deformity is indicated by his byname. 'Gam' signified that either he squinted or that he had lost an eye. A kind posterity has upheld his reputation, and for two centuries and a half the Games clan, from their great houses at Aberbrân, Newton, Tregaer, Buckland and Penderyn were prominent in Brecknock affairs as sheriffs, recorders, parliamentary representatives, justices of the peace, bailiffs and mayors. Further, through the marriage of his daughter Gwladus to Sir William ap Thomas of Raglan, Dafydd was to be the ancestor of all the Herberts. Sadly, the male line was to die out with Hoo Games in 1657.

Newton: an ancestral home of the Games' family

NOTES

[1] Einion the Englishman.
[2] Richard the tall.
[3] Cal. of Close Rolls, 79.
[4] £26 13s. 4d.
[5] This story did not gain currency until the time of Robert Vaughan of Hengwrt in the latter half of the seventeenth century.
[6] Steward.
[7] Cal. Pat. Rolls, 406.
[8] £466 13s. 4d.
[9] Smith, L.T. (ed.), *Leland's Itinerary in England and Wales*, Vol. 3, p. 108.
[10] The English dead amounted to about 1,600. The French, on the other hand, may have lost as many as 6,000. Among the dead, also, was Dafydd's son-in-law, Roger Fychan of Brodorddyn.

SIR JOHN PRICE (1502?-1555)

Sir John Price was born *c*. 1502 the son of Rhys ap Gwilym and his wife, Gwenllian, who was the daughter of one Hywel Madog. Lineally, he was descended from one of the oldest families in the county of Brecknock—he could trace his descent back to Dafydd Gam of Agincourt fame[1]—and the poet Hywel ap Dafydd ap Ieuan ap Rhys, the family bard at the great house of Raglan, was related to him. Throughout a comparatively short life he was to maintain a close relationship with the Welsh bardic tradition.

Details about his early life are few and far between but it is reasonable to postulate that he aspired to a career at law, one of the more attractive and lucrative professions open to the sons of gentlemen. It is fairly certain that he was the John Pryse who obtained the degree of B.C.L. at Oxford on 29 February 1523-4, and the 'Apprise' who was admitted to the Middle Temple on 5 November 1523.

In the 1530s he entered the service of Thomas Cromwell, Henry VIII's chief minister, to whom he was shortly to be linked by marriage. On 11 October 1534, at Cromwell's house in Islington, he married Johan, the daughter of John Williamson whose wife, also a Johan, was sister to Cromwell's wife, Elizabeth. There was a considerable age difference between the bride and groom—common enough in Tudor times—for she was eighteen and he thirty-two. It proved a fruitful union as, altogether, they had ten children, five sons and five daughters. While the first four children were born in London between 1535-14 February 1538-9, the younger offspring were all born in Hereford. The eldest son, Gregory, who was Price's principal heir, was born on 6 August 1535 and was named after Cromwell's son, his godfather. He was to become sheriff of Brecknock on two occasions, 1588 (Armada Year) and 1595. His four other sons were named Richard, so called after his godfather Richard Williams, Cromwell's nephew, John, William and Bartholomew. The daughters were called Elinor, so named after the wife of Christopher Barker, Garter King of Arms, Joan, Jane, Ursula and Mary. He had another daughter, Gomond, but she was illegitimate.[2] Joan, who was born on 14 November 1542, took as her second husband Thomas Jones (Twm Siôn Cati, *c.* 1530-1609) with whose name so many tales of an apocryphal nature are linked.[3] The names of the godparents of the elder children demonstrate how Sir John had influential friends in London, while the godparents of those born in Hereford were of the kind that a county and cathedral town could provide: a dean of the cathedral, a canon, the wife of a mayor, and members of local armorial families. In his will he made provision for all. His numerous bequests included money for the marriage of his daughters, but Dame Johan, his widow, and his eldest sons, Gregory and Richard, inherited the bulk of the landed estates, Gregory, in due course to inherit his estates in Herefordshire, while Richard was to inherit those in Brecknock. Sir John, as befitted his exalted situation in life, was the proud possessor of costly raiments, and his gowns—some faced with velvet—jackets, doublets and caps were valuable assets and worthy to be bequeathed to relatives and friends. Also bequeathed were his chain of gold and his rings.

Through his patron Cromwell he soon came to the King's notice, and from being one of Cromwell's officials, he became a royal servant and agent and he was to serve his sovereign well. When Henry, having 'divorced' his first wife, Catherine of Aragon, for failing to provide him with a male heir married, as his second wife, Anne Boleyn, 'one of the French Queen's women', John Price acted as one of the servitors. Later, ironically, he was to be involved in Henry's divorce from Anne on the grounds of her manifold adulteries, one of her alleged lovers being her own brother. Following her execution Sir John became immersed in arrangements for the marriage of the King to Jane Seymour, the wife with whom Henry was to be uniquely happy, and who was to bear him a male heir, Edward, the future Edward VI.

In the 1530s the King and Thomas Cromwell organised the sovereign nation state, and amongst the changes necessary to achieve this desirable end were the repudiation of papal authority and the dissolution of the monasteries. By the Act of Supremacy 1534 centuries of jurisdiction over the church from Rome were abruptly brought to an end, and the King was elevated to the position of 'Supreme Head on Earth of the Church of England'. Sir John Price was happy enough to accept this new and revolutionary situation and on 23 October 1535, as chancellor of the University of Cambridge, he took the oath acknowledging Henry's new status. However, there were clerics and laymen of distinction within the Kingdom who were less than happy with this breach with tradition, and refused to take the oath. Amongst these were a bishop like John Fisher and a scholar like Sir Thomas More, the author of *Utopia*. Sir John Price, in his capacity as Notary Public and Principal Registrar of the King in ecclesiastical causes, was engaged not only in recording and attesting documents relating to the abrogation of papal authority, he also took the testimonies and confessions of dissidents like Fisher and More.

The dissolution of the monasteries was achieved between 1536-40. In 1536 all those religious houses with an annual income of less than £200 were dissolved, while between 1538-40 the larger remaining ones disappeared. The monasteries had to go, because they were bastions of papal authority, and the King, who was perennially short of money because of such factors as inflation and costly wars, coveted their wealth. They had also very largely outlived their usefulness, and evils and abuses had crept in. In 1535 commissioners visited the religious houses to inquire into the state of the morals and the quality of the religious life of the inmates, and they were given to understand that their main function was to find grounds which would justify dissolution. Sir John Price was appointed one of these visitors. Though these visitors have been described as unprincipled, Sir John, perhaps, should not be judged too harshly, for he had some sympathy with the monastic ideal. His reports were mild, and he even praised the monasteries, especially the nunneries, for their educational work. He is believed not to have visited any of the Welsh houses, though a letter which he wrote on behalf of the erudite abbot of Neath abbey, Leyshon Thomas, has survived. Neath abbey, which had established a considerable reputation for itself as a centre of learning, 'universi Nedd'[4] according to the bards, had been spared from dissolution in 1536 on payment of a substantial fine of £150 and Sir John in his missive informs us that the abbot had 'of late dangered himself and his friends very far with the reclamation of the house'. Leyshon's efforts to save his house proved of little avail and in 1539 Neath also joined the list of roofless abbeys. In November 1539 Sir John had signed the surrender of Bury St Edmunds and between 9 December-27 January, in company with other commissioners, he had visited monasteries in the west of England, an itinerary which began at Bristol and ended at Evesham.

Sir John Price's experiences as a monastic 'visitor', together with his intimacy with Cromwell, the chief architect of the dissolution of the monasteries and the breach with Rome, meant that he was in possession of the vital inside information, and the 'pull' at court, which placed him at a tremendous advantage in relation to others when it came to the disposition of the dissolved lands of the monasteries. He capitalised on these advantages to acquire possession of the lands and buildings of the Benedictine Priory of St John the Evangelist at Brecon when it was dissolved in 1538. The priory had managed to survive beyond 1536 because it was a dependent house of Battle Abbey in Sussex, which was surrendered that year. He converted part of the conventual buildings into a dwelling for himself, and here he lived until 1540, when he removed to Hereford. Hugh Thomas, the Breconshire Herald, writing in 1698, describes the Priory House in these words: 'adjoining to which (the parish church of St John) is the Priory nothing inferior to the Church which for its Greatness and Inclosures of strong em-walls looks more like a Town separate from the other than the House of a private Gentleman having no less than three Great Gates for Entrance into the outward Court'. This house boasted a magnificent library since, in addition to his own collection, Sir John acquired possession of most of the books and manuscripts belonging to the priory, many the products of the famous scriptorium located there. On his decease the library was dispersed, though by then it had probably been removed to his home in Hereford. His Welsh books were left to Thomas Vaughan of Glamorgan, his manuscripts of divinity to

Hereford Cathedral, and his manuscripts of histories and humanities to his second son, Richard. Amongst the histories were William of Malmebury's *De Regibus Anglorum* and *Henricus Huntington*. The printed books in his possession, with the exception of the works of 'Saint Austen and course of the canon law' which were given to the vicar of Bromyard, were to be divided between Gregory and Richard. Some of the manuscripts which belonged to him are now in repositories as disparate as the National Library of Wales, Aberystwyth, the Bodleian Library, Oxford, the FitzWilliam Library, Cambridge, and the British Library. In Balliol College Library there is a manuscript in his own hand containing transcripts of Welsh poetry including eulogies addressed to him by bards like Lewis Morgannwg, Thomas Vaughan and Griffith Hiraethog. Included also are a Welsh bardic grammar, some proverbs and other miscellanea.

Sir John as a member of an old, well-established Brecknock landed family had greatly augmented his broad acres by his acquisition of the lands of Brecon Priory. That he was possessed

Priory House: as it is today

of more than a passing acquaintance with the soil is made abundantly clear in his introduction to *Yny Lhyvyr Hwnn*.[5] In his preface he provided guidance, doubtless based on long practical experience, on the routine to be followed with regard to the sowing and harvesting of crops during the farming year. Thus oats, peas and beans were to be sown in February and March; barley, flax and hemp in April, and wheat and rye in May. The reaping and harvesting were tasks for the warm summer months. Haymaking was to take place in June and July, and the reaping of wheat, oats, rye and barley between August and October. November, as a comparatively slack month, could be devoted to the felling of ash trees to be used for the making of ploughs.

Brecon could count itself fortunate that, unlike many of the other religious houses in Wales, the Priory of St John the Evangelist was never reduced to a heap of rubble. The priory was saved from that fate because during the Middle Ages the monastic church had served a dual purpose: while one section was given over to the devotions of the monks, the other served as a parish church, the two parts being separated by a most impressive screen three, or even four, storeys high.

Together with being a notable lawyer and an efficient civil servant, Sir John was also a renowned humanist, a disciple of the great Dutch scholar, Erasmus. He was very critical of the deficiencies of the Welsh clergy, and it was to compensate for these failings that he published in 1546, at his own expense, *Yny Lhyvyr Hwnn*, the printer being Edward Whitchurch. The church in Wales was certainly in need of reform. The higher clergy, especially the bishops, were invariably English and appointed for political services rendered to the Crown. Considering the unattractiveness of the Welsh dioceses—their remoteness, their isolation and their poverty—it is hardly surprising that these English bishops rarely visited them, with a consequent neglect of diocesan duties and obligations. What they sought was a quick translation to wealthier sees in England, and they consequently regarded their Welsh sees simply as stepping stones along that route. Between these absentee English bishops and the lower clergy, who were recruited from the ranks of native society and

Yny Lhyvyr Hwnn: frontispiece

were Welsh in speech and sympathy, there existed an unbridgeable divide. Not much is known about these parish priests. Since the fatter livings were to be found in England, the better educated amongst them were inevitably attracted there. Those that remained to labour in the Welsh vineyard were poorly educated and badly remunerated with stipends that varied between five and fifteen pounds a year. This poverty compelled them to become pluralists, and consequently guilty of absenteeism, though it has to be remembered that these evils were not exclusive to them. Again, many of the clergy, both high and low, deliberately flouted the Catholic law of celibacy, as many kept wives and cocubines quite openly. There were some forty-three married priests in the Bangor diocese alone.

Yny Lhyvyr Hwnn was in the nature of an instructional manual designed to provide guidance to the lower clergy to enable them to conduct the services properly. According to Sir John the lower clergy 'either cannot or will not reveal to their parishioners those things which it is the duty of the one to teach and the other to learn'. As a result of this failure in communication large numbers of his fellow countrymen lay 'in the direst darkness, lacking a knowledge of God and the commandments and thereby falling into greater depth of sins and vices than other nations'. The content of the book embraced the creed, the lord's prayer and the commandments, though the eighth commandment, 'Thou shalt not steal', was significantly omitted.[6] It could be that Sir John, as a humanist scholar of considerable stature, was too critical of the deficiencies of the lower clergy, and that he had set his sights too high for the average incumbent. On the other hand, Sir John went to considerable pains to stress that his book was intended not for scholars, but for the unlearned. The content of the book represented the very least which every priest in the Middle Ages was expected to teach his flock. To the vast majority of these the essential teachings of the church were but dimly apprehended. For them religion was something to be administered on their behalf by the priest.

The book was certainly significant as a religous primer; but it also represented a beginning to the task of satisfying the needs of a mainly monoglot Welsh-speaking population for the scriptures to be translated into the mother tongue. Hitherto the gospels had been presented to them in a medium which was entirely incomprehensible to them—Latin. For that matter it was not understood by many of the lower clergy either. Now a pioneering attempt was made by Sir John to lighten their darkness by translating parts of the scriptures at least into the vernacular language. It was in this rather humble manner that a development, which was to culminate in the complete translation of the bible into Welsh by Bishop William Morgan in 1588, was inaugurated. Sir John is to be numbered among the first Welshmen to appreciate the importance of the printing press; he realised how much more effective than manuscripts the printed book was in spreading literary texts in the native language. He further recognised that there were Welshmen who could only read their own language and no other.

Sir John was now to be involved with a policy which was to have very far reaching effects on Wales despite the fact that, in some respects, Henry VIII and Cromwell were only giving legal recognition to trends which were already at work. In 1536 the Act of Union between England and Wales was passed, and this was supplemented by another measure in 1543 which filled in the details of that settlement, the bare bones of which had been laid down in 1536. Many motives have been attributed for the passing of these acts: there was the need to arrive at some kind of solution to the endemic disorders in Welsh society; the breach with Rome had made Wales vulnerable to invasion from abroad, and Henry VIII may well have been imbued with Renaissance ideas concerning the nature of Kingship, and particularly by the notion that a King should seek to augment his power and authority in every possible way. However, a crucial factor at work was the demand for union from within Wales herself, and particularly from the progressive middle class element of landed gentry of which Sir John was a representative. In Lord Herbert of Cherbury's *Life of Henry VIII* there is preserved a petition craving for the Welsh 'to be received and adopted into the same laws and privileges which your other subjects enjoy'. The petitioners claimed that despite the earlier loyalty of the Welsh to the Yorkists, they had long since been loyal to the Tudors, and they begged for union as a reward for this loyalty. It is quite possible that Sir John was the author of this petition. He was certainly a key adviser to the government on Welsh affairs, and in this case he may very well have been put up to it by his kinsman by marriage, Thomas Cromwell, the King's chief minister, and the royal official mainly responsible for the union policy designed principally to consolidate England's position as a sovereign nation state. Sir John was warm in his praise of the policy enshrined in this legislation, and he referred to Henry as a prince 'as godly as he is powerful. And since he has already bestowed on the Welsh nation so many temporal blessings he will be no less willing to allow them spiritual gifts'.

In 1540, following the fall of Cromwell, Sir John was made secretary to the Council in Wales and the Marches which had its centre at Ludlow. His peripatetic days were over. The Council exercised functions both of an administrative and judicial nature over the thirteen shires of Wales, together with the five neighbouring English shires.[7] The secretary was, undoubtedly, the most powerful and senior of all its officials. He was always a member of the Council, and he was bound to be in continual attendance at Ludlow. Though his duties are nowhere clearly defined, presumably he acted as a confidential assistant to the lord president, and was responsible for the administrative work of the Council. His salary amounted to twenty marks[8] per annum together with fees and emoluments. Sir John was to retain this highly prestigious, and possibly most lucrative, post until the time of his death. Immediately after his appointment he was involved in a dispute with Charles Fox who, with his brother Edmund, held the post of clerk of the signet and clerk of the council, over their respective roles. The matter was referred to the Privy Council in London but the outcome is not known.

Royal favour meant that posts fell into his lap like ripe apples. In 1534 he was made registrar of Salisbury Cathedral; he was included on commissions of the peace in Monmouthshire and the marcher shires; in 1546 he was placed on the chantry commissions of both north and south Wales, and on commissions for church plate and properties in Herefordshire in 1552-3. He became sheriff of Brecknock in 1543, and of Herefordshire in 1554. Lands, also, came his way. Apart from Brecon Priory, he obtained leases of the rectory of Llanfihangel Iorath in Carmarthenshire in 1536-7, and he was able first to lease (8 June 1540), and afterwards, on 13 November 1542, to purchase the dissolved priory of St Guthlac, a cell of Gloucester abbey, in the suburbs of Hereford. St Guthlac then became his principal residence and a beloved home, 'nunc mihi adoptiua est patria, ideogue carissima.⁹ In recognition of his dedicated services to the Crown, on Shrove Tuesday 1547, two days after the coronation of Edward VI, a knighthood was conferred on him.

During the sixteenth century as Parliament, and particularly the House of Commons, acquired a vastly enhanced authority as an instrument of government, a seat in the lower house became increasingly coveted by the gentry. Sir John was fully conversant with the workings of that constitutional arrangement whereby the King worked through Parliament, an institution beloved by Cromwell, which had the effect of doubling the constitutional importance of that body. A seat in that assemblage had become most desirable and so, in 1547, he was returned for Brecknockshire, an indication of his social standing in that shire. He appears next in the first three Marian Parliaments. In October 1553 he sat for Hereford, where he had his main residence, and in this Parliament he was not to oppose the legislation designed to effect the restoration of Catholicism. At the next election, his position as sheriff of Herefordshire compelled him to look elsewhere for a seat, and since he worked at Ludlow, he used his position and connections there to provide himself with one. However, it would appear that it was a contested election as the indenture bears an alteration suggestive of this. Six months later he entered his last Parliament only by filling a vacancy caused when Anthony Browne, who had been elected for both Maldon and Ludgershall, chose to represent Maldon. At the by-election held on 19 November 1554, seven days after the opening of Parliament, Sir John replaced him at Ludgershall, a victory which he owed to the influence which Sir Richard Brydges was able to exert. This Parliament witnessed the repeal of the Act of Supremacy by which Henry VIII had become head of the Church of England, and Sir John was not found to be absent at this critical vote.

But while great events were unfolding around him in which he was, in a real sense, a participant, Sir John still found time to enter with enthusiasm into the furore provoked by Polydore Vergil's attack on Geoffrey of Monmouth. Geoffrey in his *Historia Regum Britanniae* had argued for a glorious British past. He conceived of a powerful empire having been established in Britain by Brutus and his Trojan followers, and he detailed the mighty deeds of their descendants down to the time of Cadwaladr (d. A.D. 664). This mythical account had been enthusiastically received in Wales for it enabled the Welsh to maintain that they were descended from the oldest and most celebrated inhabitants of the island. This illustrious lineage, in turn, conferred on them the right to regard themselves as the rightful rulers of the whole of Britain. The Italian Polydore Vergil, in his criticism of Geoffrey, argued that if there had been such a glorious empire in early Britain, why was it that classical authors had made no reference to it. However, Geoffrey had no shortage of champions who were prepared to enter the lists on his behalf, and one of the most skilful and learned of these was Sir John Price. An early draft of his defence, written before 1545, is preserved, but before the death of Edward VI (1553) he had composed a further reply. In his will he charged his second son, Richard, eighteen at the time, with its publication, a task which he accomplished in 1573 under the title *Historiae Britannicae Defensio*. Sir John also wrote a description of Cambria in Latin which was subsequently translated into English by Humphrey Llwyd, the noted antiquary and physician (1527-68). This translation became the basis of *The Historie of Cambria now called Wales* published in 1584 by David Powel, a cleric and historian of considerable merit. A treatise in manuscript form on the restoration of the coinage, and dedicated to Mary Tudor, is also attributed to him.

Though Sir John had ceased to be domiciled in Brecon some time after 1540, his affection for his native town, where he had served as bailiff in 1544-5, was exemplified in his will, where two bequests were made for the benefit of the borough and its less fortunate inhabitants. In one he left £10 towards the repair of the bridge over the river Usk, the money to be expended at the discretion of the bailiff and his 'two oldest brethren'. He further gave an additional £20, which the bailiff and his two colleagues were to distribute 'among the poor householders there and poor maidens' marriages'.

On 15 October 1555 Sir John died at his home in Hereford aged fifty-three. Historian, antiquary, lawyer, classical scholar, theologian, he was all these rolled into one. But his interests were still broader. English orthography and phonetics also captured his attention. The lamentable state of English orthography in the early sixteenth century was referred to at the beginning of the *Defensio* where Sir John recounts how he experimented by inviting four educated Englishmen, skilled in the written word, to write English sentences at his dictation. They all used different spellings. How different, he averred, was the condition of orthography in Wales where ten educated Welshmen would spell in Welsh in exactly the same way. He noted that the vowels in Welsh were the same as the vowels in Greek but different from those in Latin.

Sir John passed away an extremely wealthy man. In his will, made on 6 October 1555, he recorded that he had delivered 1,000 marks[10] to the keeping and custody of Thomas Havard 'whereof £500 is in gold and fine silver and locked in a coffer or chest under three locks, the three keys whereof I will that three of my executors hereafter named do have the keeping'. Together with these liquid assets, he had lands in his possession to the value of about £135 a year. His final wish—and he was to die nine days later—was that he should be buried in the cathedral church of Hereford. A great light had gone out, and though his bones lie interred outside his native heath he was, and will always remain, a great son of Wales.

NOTES

[1] Supra, pp. 13-18

[2] The fact that Gomond was married to James Gomond, one of the executors of the will, has led to the belief that Sir John must have been married twice. She is not mentioned with the other daughters, and was only left the £4 which her mother 'had borrowed' from Sir John.

[3] He hailed from Fountain Gate, near Tregaron, and was the son of a Cardiganshire gentleman. Joan was his second wife. He was possessed of some scholarship and was a bard to boot.

[4] University of Neath. The bard in question was Lewis Morgannwg.

[5] In this Book. The title page is missing and so the work is known by the first words of the text.

[6] He was the one who had gained possession of the dissolved lands of St John the Evangelist.

[7] These were Hereford, Gloucester, Worcester, Shropshire and Cheshire.

[8] £266 8s.

[9] Now the idea of my adopted country is most dear to me.

[10] £13,333 4s.

JOHN PENRY (1563-93)

Mae'r wirffydd eto yn y tir
A geraist ti goruwch bob gwlad,
A gloyw lamp ym Methel wan
A llafar gloch mewn llawer llan. [1]

Crwys

In 1558 Elizabeth I, at the age of twenty-five, ascended the English throne. She succeeded to a throne surrounded by 'snares and challenges, domestic and foreign', [2] but fortunately for the kingdom, she was possessed of wisdom far beyond her years, and she had also learnt from the mistakes of her half-sister, Mary Tudor; mistakes which she was determined never to repeat. Amongst the most pressing and immediate of her problems at home was the resolution of the religious question, as the country had experienced violent oscillations in governmental policy since Henry VIII's breach with Rome in 1534. During the reign of his delicate son, Edward VI, Protestantism had replaced Catholicism as the state religion. However, during the reign of Edward's successor, Mary I, Catholicism had been restored, together with the authority of the Pope, with the result that in 1558 the country was split between two opposing minority religious groups, the convinced Protestants on the one hand, and the reformed Catholics on the other, and in between was the largely inert mass of the people waiting to be saved by the one group or the other.

Elizabeth, fully aware that she had to walk warily, in 1559 drew up her settlement of religion, by which the Protestant Anglican Church was established. This settlement was based on two statutary enactments: the Act of Supremacy and the Act of Uniformity. By the former, papal authority was once more removed and Elizabeth accorded the rather grandiose title of 'Supreme Governor of all things temporal and spiritual'; the latter enforced the use of the second English Book of Common Prayer 1552 with slight modifications. The Queen herself would have preferred the adoption of the more moderate book of 1549, but the pressure from Protestant sympathisers, and especially the Puritan exiles newly returned from Frankfurt and Geneva, the Coxians[3] and the Knoxians,[4] compelled her to move much further in a Protestant direction than she had originally intended. In 1563 the settlement was rounded off with the passing of the articles of faith of the new church, the Thirty-Nine Articles.

Though the settlement of 1559 was essentially a compromise, a kind of *via media* between the Queen's religious views and those of her Protestant subjects represented on the benches of the House of Commons, there were groups within the kingdom which were resolutely opposed to it from its very inception: the Catholics and the Puritans. The Catholics opposed it because it was Protestant and anti-papal; the Puritans because it was not radical enough. Catholic survivals in worship such as making the sign of the cross, and bowing at the name of Jesus, were anathema to them, and they were even to attack the organisation of the church and particularly its episcopal structure, which the extremer elements wanted to destroy 'root and branch'. But despite their criticisms of what they perceived to be its many imperfections, like the lack of clerical education, and pluralism, non-residence and simony, the majority of Puritans during Elizabeth's reign, very much like the Methodists in the eighteenth century, were to be found within the framework of the church. However, the church did not contain them all, and one who was to adopt a position outside it was a Brecknockshire man, John Penry.

Penry was born in 1563 on the northern slopes of the Epynt mountain, the son of a fairly prosperous farmer, Meredith Penry, of Cefn Brith, near Llangamarch. His father's family, the Penrys of Llwyncyntefin or Old Grove, was one of the oldest in Brecknockshire. The house in which he first saw the light of day was a typical Welsh long house with humans and cattle sharing the same thatched roof, the humans at the top end and the animals at the lower. He probably received his early education at the hands of the local clergyman because it is well-established that many of the clergy, in order to supplement their meagre incomes, were teachers as well as ministers. The priest, in a school held possibly in the parish church at Llangamarch, could well have taught him to read and write English, as well as imparting to him some knowledge of Latin grammar. Following this initial instruction, it is probable that Penry gained admission to Christ College, Brecon, the first of the Tudor endowed grammar schools to be established in Wales (1541). After all, the school was situated only some fifteen miles from his home at Cefn Brith. The curriculum at Christ College would have been heavily weighted in favour of the teaching of Latin grammar and literature, together with a little Greek, and some provision for religious education. No room was given to the teaching of mathematics and foreign languages, and there were few opportunities for playing games. Since William Barlow, the bishop of St David's encouraged it, a little time might have been devoted to singing. The medium of instruction was English, and the use of Welsh was actively discouraged. For scholars like Penry the daily regimen was hard. Work began at six a.m. and the school day was of eight hours' duration, with breaks for breakfast and lunch and one afternoon free. Discipline was very severe, and to help enforce it, senior boys were appointed as monitors. During his years at the school, Penry may well have been struck by one of these since this was certainly the experience of boys at Rhuthun. The emphasis on Latin arose in large measure from vocational need, as it was inconceivable that

Cefn Brith, Llangamarch, birthplace of John Penry

anyone should enter any ecclesiastical, diplomatic or legal post unless he was conversant with that tongue. The primary purpose of the school, however, was the inculcation of the virtue of obedience to church and state, to king, bishop, priest and magistrate. The lesson was not lost on Penry, for throughout his brief career he was to profess his deep loyalty to the Queen.

Following his early school education, Penry, at the age of seventeen, entered Peterhouse College, Cambridge, where he spent the next four years. He matriculated on 11 June 1580, and on 21 March 1584 he graduated B.A. At this time Welshmen, desirous of a university education, had to leave their native heath as there were no such institutions in Wales.[5] His parents were so supportive of his ambitions that at Cambridge he did not have to wait at graduates' tables in order to earn his keep, as poor students then were constrained to do. He paid for his board and lodging, and was not stinted in his expenditure. His name does not appear in the college records for 1585, and it is probable that he had returned to Wales, and was devoting his time to preaching to his fellow countrymen. Certainly, his detailed knowledge of the great famine caused by the failure of the harvests in that year suggests that he may have experienced this at first hand. His preaching was so melodious that he was called *Telyn Cymru* (The Welsh Harp). His experiences in Wales impressed upon him the ignorance of the people where the Bible was concerned, and the need for a preaching ministry. He now returned to university, but to Oxford rather than Cambridge. At Oxford—which had always attracted more students from Wales than Cambridge—under the protection of the all-powerful Earl of Leicester, the Puritans were not only tolerated but encouraged. Since they were influential at Cambridge also, it was inevitable that Penry should have been brought into contact with Presbyterian thinkers at both universities. He was to be a post-graduate student at St Albans Hall, Oxford, from 28 May 1586 until he obtained his masters degree on 11 July.

It was at Cambridge, however, that Penry underwent a profound religious experience which was to determine his whole future career. He speaks of himself as one who 'had known a

remission of our sins, even of our great sins'. In theology Penry
was a Calvinist, and he believed implicitly in the authority of the
scriptures. To Penry 'merely to be ignorant of the redemptive
mercy of God as presented in Christ was to be eternally damned'.
He was never to take orders, and on no occasion did he question
the validity of the sacraments. Like the great German Protestant
reformer, Martin Luther, he believed in salvation by faith alone,
and to attain this state people had to be convinced of their sinful-
ness and this could best be accomplished by preaching to them.

Penry, as an earnest Puritan, was naturally deeply influenced
by the ignorance and low spiritual life of the people of Wales, as
exemplified by their idolatry, swearing, adultery, and thieving.
His concern led him to write three treatises: *The Aequity of an
Humble Supplication* (1587), *An Exhortation unto the Governors
and People of Her Majesty's Country of Wales* (1588), and *A
view of Some Part of Such Public Wants and Disorders as are in
the Service of God within Her Majesty's Country of Wales*
(otherwise known as *A Supplication unto the High Court of
Parliament* (1589). The *Aequity* was published at Oxford by
Joseph Barnes but as the principal market for books was
London, it was sold there at St Paul's churchyard at the sign of
the 'Tiger's Head'. He draws a gloomy picture of religious
conditions in Wales and roundly declares that non-residence had
'cut the throat of our Church. Some that never preached have
three church livings', and he implores the Queen and Parliament
to initiate measures that would be effective in bringing the light of
the gospel to the country. He requested that more preachers
should be dispatched to Wales to dispel the mists of darkness. To
help with the work, Welshmen occupying pulpits in England
could be asked to return to Wales. 'The remedy of this our
grievous case is only had, and no other way, by providing unto us
such pastors as may feed us the pure word of God'. So desperate
was the need for preachers that he even advocated that laymen
should be permitted to preach—Penry was a case in point—and
that they should be remunerated from voluntary contributions.
In this treatise he did not attack the bishops, though he was
bitterly critical of the clergy whom he variously dubbed as 'dumb

The Aequity:
John Penry's first book

A TREATISE
CONTAINING
THE AEQVITY OF
AN HVMBLE SVPPLI-
CATION WHICH IS TO BE
EXHIBITED VNTO HIR
GRACIOVS MAIESTY AND
this high Court of Parliament
in the behalfe of the Countrey of
Wales, that some order may
be taken for the preaching of
the Gospell among those
people.

Wherein also is set downe as much of the
estate of our people as without offence
could be made known, to the end that
our case (if it please God) may be piti-
ed by them who are not of this assembly, and so they also may bee driuen to
labour on our behalfe.

AT OXFORD,
Printed by IOSEPH BARNES, and are
to be sold in Pauls Church-yard at the
signe of the Tygershead. I 5 8 7.

and greedy dogs', 'rogues and vagabonds', 'spendthrifts and
serving men', 'adulterers', 'drunkards', 'thieves', 'roisterers',
and 'swearers'. They were fully deserving of these labels for
leaving the people in ignorance of the Bible. 'Thousands there be
of our people that know Jesus Christ to be neither God nor man,
king, priest nor prophet. O desolate and forlorn condition'.

There were areas in Wales where sermons were either unknown or heard once in a lifetime. His condemnation was devastating: 'My brethren for the most part know not what preaching meaneth . . . they think it sufficient to hear one sermon once perhaps in all their life'. In far too many instances the clergyman was not conversant with the Welsh language, and to Penry the preaching of the gospel in the mother tongue, to a predominantly monoglot population, by men of good character, was the only means to salvation for the Welsh people. It was imperative, therefore, that the Bible should be translated into Welsh, for only the Prayer Book and the New Testament were then available in translation, a work which had been begun in 1563 and completed on 1 March 1567 by William Salesbury, Richard Davies and Thomas Huet. However, because of peculiarities in Salesbury's orthography,[6] they had proved less suitable for public worship than they might have been.

Penry's treatise, written in the white heat of passion, was presented to Parliament on 28 February 1587 by Edward Dunn Lee, the member for the Carmarthen boroughs, and Job Throckmorton, a fervent Puritan and M.P. for Warwickshire. Parliament, however, took very little notice of it, as that body felt that it would be very difficult to implement its proposals, and the Court might find it offensive even though it was obsequious enough, and Penry did not advocate freedom of thought in religion. Rather were Pelagians, Arians and Papists to be punished as heretics. However, John Whitgift the Archbishop of Canterbury, certainly did not find it to his taste, and since in his eyes Penry had published 'flat treason and heresy' he was summoned to appear before the Court of High Commission, and invited to retract statements which he had made in the book. This Penry stoutly refused to do, declaring, 'never so long as I live, God willing'. He was now imprisoned for a month in the Gatehouse at Westminster, and by order of the court copies of his book—the original print-out was 500—were destroyed.

The lenity of the punishment is quite remarkable; possibly it was due to the fact that the Court did not wish to risk a head-on clash with Parliament. The two sponsors certainly incurred the

wrath of the authorities, Dunn being removed from the commission of the peace, and Throckmorton calling down on his head
the fury of the Queen. But Penry's barbed criticism may well have
spurred his most implacable enemy, the Archbishop, into speed-
ing up the appearance of the Welsh Bible, the work of William
Morgan, in 1588. Within weeks of summoning Penry before him,
Whitgift arranged for Morgan to come to London to hasten the
publication of his translation. Without this official support it is
doubtful whether the Welsh Bible would have appeared when it
did; it is also possible that without Whitgift's patronage and
encouragement, Morgan would have lost heart and left the translation only partly completed. Penry's release from prison
enabled him to pursue his courtship of Eleanor Godley, the
daughter of Henry Godley, a Puritan living in Northampton, and
on 5 September 1588 she became his wife. She was to bear Penry
four daughters: Deliverance, Comfort, Safety and Sure Hope.

The term of imprisonment had not, in any way, dampened
Penry's ardour, for he declared that 'since the time of my release,
I saw myself bound in conscience not to give over my former
purpose, in seeking the good of my countrymen, by the rooting
out of ignorance and blindness among them'. He now proceeded
to compose another appeal on behalf of Wales: *The Exhortation.*
Beneath the title were verses from the Psalms and from
Corinthians:

> If I shall forget thee, O Jerusalem, let my right hand forget
> herself, if I do not remember thee, let my tongue cleave unto
> the roof of my mouth: yea, if I prefer not Jerusalem unto my
> chief joy.

Joseph Barnes, the Oxford printer, had by now in all probab-
ility, been warned not to publish any more of Penry's works, and
so it had become necessary to find another printer possessed of
the physical and moral courage to defy the government. Furthermore, it had become advisable to have the work published clan-
destinely. At the beginning of 1588, Penry became involved with
the secret press of the Puritan, Robert Waldegrave, who operated
from the 'Sign of the Crane' in St Paul's churchyard. Waldegrave

had had several brushes with authority already for publishing seditious material, and had spent six months in gaol. The *Exhortation* appeared in April 1588, and, despite every effort made by the officers to apprehend the author, Penry succeeded in eluding them.

Having failed to influence Parliament, Penry now addressed himself to the Lord President (the Earl of Pembroke) and the members of the Council in the Marches of Wales at Ludlow. He returns to his theme of the provision of the Gospel in Welsh, and he rejoices at the news that William Morgan's translation is ready for printing. However, the religious condition of Wales now takes second place to aspersions about 'dumb ministers' i.e. non-preaching clergymen. He ascribes the root of the problem to the bishops and their practice of appointing unworthy priests. It was profanity for such ministers to administer the sacraments, and a sin to receive it at their hands. Ordination was not at all necessary for preaching. It was obvious that Penry had begun to depart from the doctrines of the Established Church and was veering towards Separatism. He was now fully aware that his activities and ambitions on behalf of his countrymen were imperilling his own life. Courageously he remarked that he 'came with the rope around my neck to save you ... Howsoever it goes with me, I labour that you may have the Gospel preached among you; though it cost me my life, I think it well bestowed'.

Penry now became associated with the Martin Marprelate Tracts though he always strenuously denied that he was Martin. Martin Marprelate was a pen-name, and his true identity[7] is still unknown. In his writings, using colloquial language, he mocked and satirised the bishops. He regaled his readers with scandalous tales about their private lives, which appeared an open book to him, and caused them severe embarrassment. After the appearance of the *Epistle*, the first of the Marprelate Tracts, the search for the ubiquitous press was intensified, and eventually the authorities discovered its whereabouts. At midnight officers broke into Waldegrave's shop and completely destroyed the press. The printer, however, managed to escape, taking with him, hidden under his cloak, a box of pica type. Advance warning must have been received of the impending raid, for all copies of the *Exhortation* had been removed.

Waldegrave now took the box of type to the home of a Mrs Nicholas Crane in Aldermanbury, a widow who was in complete sympathy with the goals that Penry and Waldegrave had set themselves. For the work to continue it was necessary to establish another press as soon as possible, and Penry succeeded in setting one up near Kingston-on-Thames. But the relentless search for it by the authorities meant that it had to be moved yet again, and a new home was found for it at East Molesey, a few miles from Kingston, where it was hidden in another house owned by Mrs Crane.

The press used by Penry and Waldegrave was very basic. The first printing press in England had been established at Westminster Abbey by William Caxton in 1476, and there is a print extant depicting Caxton demonstrating the new invention to King Edward IV and his Queen. The metal type was first laid on a bed. Following this the surface of the letters was inked using pads and covered with a sheet of paper. By turning a handle a downward pressure would be exerted on the paper by a flat piece of wood leaving the imprint of the letters on it. The sheets were then hung up to dry before being stitched together to form a book. The whole process was very time-consuming and it called for the exercise of a great deal of care and patience.

Mrs Crane, although by no stretch of the imagination a wilting lily, now, naturally enough, began to have cold feet, for she appreciated the consequences were the press to be found on her property. She now begged Penry and Waldegrave to remove it, and so the press, once again, had to be dismantled. It found a new sanctuary at Fawsley House, near Daventry, a mansion belonging to Sir Richard Knightley, though Sir Richard wanted it clearly understood that in the event of the press being found there, he could not in any way be implicated. The removal of the press from East Molesey near London to Fawsley in Daventry was fraught with danger. A tenant of Sir Richard's eldest son, a husbandman by the name of Jeffs, was paid fifty shillings, quite a substantial sum in those days so that he must have had a suspicion

Printing press of the kind used by John Penry

of the dangers involved, to take a load from East Molesey hidden
under a load of hay. On arrival at Fawsley House, the press was
unloaded and transferred to an attic room, though every effort
was made by Penry and Waldegrave to conceal the fact from the
servants. However, the furtive activities associated with the room
inevitably led to gossip among them, and their difficulties were
compounded by the need to entrust the stitching of the sheets to a
certain Henry Sharpe in Northampton, a man of great inquisit-
iveness and completely untrustworthy. Again the press had to be
moved and, in February 1589, it was transferred to an empty

farm house on one of Sir Richard's estates at Norton, near Daventry.

Meanwhile, the Archbishop's officers searched the home of Penry's in-laws at Northampton hoping, undoubtedly, to apprehend him there. Penry describes the incident thus: 'Richard Walton having a commission from the Archbishop and others ... came into the place of mine abode at Northampton, ransacked my study, and took away with him all such printed books and written papers as he himself thought good'. The books which Walton uncovered convinced him that Penry's behaviour was traitorous and he charged the mayor of Northampton to arrest Penry.

Sir Richard Knightley was now advised to move the migratory press again, on this occasion from Daventry to Coventry, to the home of one John Hales, a kinsman of his. The property, 'White Friars', happened to be vacant and, furthermore, it had the advantage of being situated in a secluded part of the town. Thither the press was transported by Stephen Giffard, one of Sir Richard's servants. But John Hales, fearful of being arrested as an accomplice, would not permit Waldegrave, despite the fact that it was mid-winter, to light a fire lest the smoke arising from the chimney should disclose his presence. Waldegrave was now feeling the strain of a fugitive's existence. After all he had a wife and six children to support, and he decided to sever his connection with the press.

Waldegrave was replaced by John Hodgkins and two assistants, Thomlyn and Simms, from London, but before printing could be resumed, the press was on the move again. It was transferred to Wolston Priory, the home of Roger Wigston, situated mid-way between Coventry and Rugby. However, Hodgkins was far from happy with the new location, and so the press was conveyed to Warrington, near Manchester. At Warrington, as it was being unloaded from the cart, some type fell to the ground, and this mishap led to speculation among the onlookers who were not satisfied with the explanation that what they had seen was shot. Word reached the authorities, and the press was discovered. Hodgkins and his assistants were taken into custody and dispatched to London where, despite being tortured in the Tower, they refused to reveal the identities of their associates. Meanwhile, Henry Sharpe, the Northampton bookbinder, had been apprehended and, to save his own skin, made a full confession. As a result Sir Richard Knightley, John Hales and Roger Wigston and his wife were all imprisoned, and Penry and Waldegrave, to avoid sharing with them 'a bed of short and musty straw' were forced, in September 1589, to flee to Scotland.

It was while the press was thus wandering from one secret hiding place to another that Penry produced his *Supplication* and the *Appellation*—both in 1589. In the *Supplication* Penry petitioned Parliament to deal with the 'public wants' of Wales. One was the preaching of the Gospel. He repeated his claim that the Gospel had not been preached in Wales since the days of popery. Unless something was done the whole nation would perish, 'to live in hell for evermore'. The second 'public need' was the reform of church government. Episcopacy was not sanctioned by Scripture and, consequently, it could not possibly be defended. He would also eliminate the 'cap, surplice, tippet and other beggarly and popish ceremonies'. This was the outburst of a Presbyterian. In the *Appellation* he makes another appeal to Parliament. He complains that he is being subjected to 'bad and injurious dealing' at the hands of the Archbishop of Canterbury and the Court of High Commission for no other reason than that of writing about the state of religion in Wales. He now wishes to submit himself and his cause 'unto the determination of this honourable assembly: craveth nothing else, but either release from trouble and persecution, or just trial'. He concludes by imploring that august assembly for its protection: 'Mine only hope is in you, be not unmerciful and pitiless towards me'.

Penry was to remain in Scotland for three years. He was joined there by his wife, Eleanor, who travelled to Edinburgh from Northampton leaving their daughter, Deliverance, with her grandparents. Whitgift's spies soon established that their quarry had fled north, and when it was brought to the ears of the Queen that her kinsman James VI had granted asylum to a fugitive from English justice, she was furious. In a letter to James she beseeches him 'not to give more harbour to vagabond traitors, but to return them to me or banish them from your land'.

James VI, who had aspirations to the English throne—Elizabeth, after all, was his cousin and a virgin Queen—proclaimed Penry an outlaw, and he was given ten days to leave Scotland. Meanwhile, it was forbidden to provide him with food, drink and shelter. However, Penry's Presbyterian friends remained true, and it was not until 1592 that he left the country and then of his own accord. North of the border Penry's pen was not to remain idle, for on 8 February 1589 Richard Bancroft, an ecclesiastical commissioner, and the man in charge of a kind of sixteenth-century intelligence service to track down Puritans, had preached a sermon at St Paul's Cross which caused grave offence in Scotland as it contained a vitriolic attack on Presbyterianism. Penry's reply, in 1590, was contained in *A Brief Discovery*, and this treatise is important as it demonstrates that Penry, at this stage, was still a Presbyterian, despite his earlier teetering towards Separatism.

In 1592 Penry decided to leave the comparative safety of Scotland, where he was leading a rather furtive existence sheltered by his friends, and return to London. He declared that he was motivated to take this fateful decision by his love of Wales and his need to perform some service for her: 'It hath been my purpose always to employ my small talent in my poor country of Wales, where I know that the poor people perish for want of knowledge, and that was the only cause of my coming forth of that country where I was and might have stayed privily all my life'. However, it is questionable whether this assertion can be taken at face value. Penry, possibly, was being economical with the truth. His real reason for leaving Scotland may well lie in another direction. Penry by this time had abandoned his Presbyterian beliefs and come to share the views of the Separatists. As a result there were now huge differences between him and his Scottish brethren regarding church government and discipline. It is here that one should seek the key to the decision to return south. Towards the end of August he left Edinburgh for London, arriving at the capital early in September. In Scotland, Eleanor Penry had given birth to two girls, Comfort and Safety, and presumably the father made arrangements for his wife—who was in a delicate state of health—and daughters to travel by sea from Leith to the Thames thus obviating the necessity of journeying to London over rough and treacherous roads.

In the capital the whole family was soon reunited as Deliverance joined her parents from Northampton. There was now a further increase in the family as Eleanor was delivered of yet another child, a girl, Sure Hope, at Christmas. In the City Penry joined a group of Separatists, the followers of Henry Barrow and John Greenwood, both of whom had already been imprisoned. This sect promulgated doctrines that were subversive of the church and the royal supremacy, for they held that every congregation of Christian men formed a separate church. It is small wonder that the authorities made every effort to suppress them. Their activities were clandestine, and they worshipped in any place which offered protection from prying eyes—houses, ships, forests. In March 1593, on a Sunday morning, while a number of Separatists were gathering for worship in Islington Woods, officers appeared and arrested a large number of them, including Penry. They were removed to the house of the arresting constable, but in the general confusion Penry managed to escape, and he remained at large for three weeks under the name of John Harrison (an anglicised form of Penry). He finally came to rest in the home of a friend called Lewes in Stepney, but the vicar of the parish, one Anthony Anderson, betrayed his whereabouts and, on 22 March, he was arrested at Ratcliffe and imprisoned in the Poultry Compter. There he was held in close confinement. He was kept apart from all the other prisoners and placed in chains. Following his decision to leave Scotland he had been at liberty for only six months.

Penry remained a prisoner at the Poultry Compter for over two months, and despite the restrictions imposed upon him by his chains, he managed to pen letters to William Cecil, the Lord High Treasurer, and to his wife and family. Since his wife was not permitted to visit him, the writing materials, the quill, ink and paper, must have been smuggled into the prison, and this could only have been accomplished through the connivance of the gaoler, one Gittens. Possibly his heart had been softened by the tinkling of silver. In a letter which Penry composed to his wife on 6 April 1593, and she is always uppermost in his thoughts, he is full of grim foreboding as well as being solicitous after her welfare. He desired that his daughters should be raised by Eleanor in the knowledge of God:

> And what shift soever you make, keep our poor children with you that you may bring them up yourself in the instruction of the Lord. I leave you and them, indeed, nothing in this life but the blessing of my God and His blessed promises. I know, my good Helen, that the burden I leave upon thee of four infants, whereof the eldest is not four years old, will not seem burdensome unto thee. Yea, thou shalt find that our God will (be) a Father to the fatherless and a stay unto the widow.

He is very concerned about her spiritual wellbeing. She should spend her time in prayer and meditation and God would provide. Having related the manner of his capture and his subsequent interrogation by his captors, and having sent fond remembrances to his mother (his father must have died by this time), brother and sisters in Wales, he implores her to perform yet another service:

> I would wish you to go to the judges for me with your children, desiring them to consider your hard case and mine. Yea, and I would have you, if you can, go to the queen with them, beseeching her for God's cause, to show her wonted clemency unto her subjects—with my Lord Treasurer and others of the Council—to regard your and mine cries: for sure my life is sought for.

In a subsequent letter to his wife it is evident that he is still concerned about her welfare and that of his children, and he cherishes the hope that his family are making provision against the future:

> I will write unto them, if I can by any means, for this purpose. This is a cold and a poor stay I leave you and my

poor fatherless mess: but my God and yours, doubt you not, will provide abundantly for you and them, if you serve him, as I doubt not but you will.

On 10 April, Penry wrote a letter to his children in which he addresses them not as children but as adults. He exhorts them to be kind to the people of his native land and particularly to his family there:

Show kindness unto the kindred whereof you have come but especially if ever you are able, show all forwardness in doing good unto my people and kindred in the flesh, and be always ready to show yourselves helpful unto the least child of that poor country, that shall stand in need of your loving support. In any case, repay the kindness, if you be able, which I owe unto my nearest kindred there, as to my Mother, Brethren, Sisters, etc who I am persuaded will be most kind towards you and your Mother ... And be an especial comfort in my stead, unto the grey hairs of my poor Mother, whom the Lord used as the only means of my stay for me in my beginning up at my studies.

His sole wealth was four Bibles, and these he bequeathed to his daughters, one for each, and he charges them to read their copies by day and by night.

Eleanor Penry, in obedience to her husband's wishes, now petitioned Sir John Puckering, Lord Keeper of Her Majesty's Great Seal of England. She begged to be allowed access to her husband in prison and to provide him with some of the comforts of life. He was very weak and sickly and his gaoler only allowed him bread and drink: 'If he were the veriest traitor that ever was, it is not her Majesty's pleasure that he should thus be hardly used'. The accusation that Penry was being ill-treated was taken seriously, and officers were sent to the Poultry Compter to investigate the allegations though Eleanor was still debarred from visiting her husband. However, Eleanor herself was now committed to the Gatehouse prison by the Lord Chief Justice though, somehow, she managed to make good her escape.

Meantime, Penry had written a letter in which he excuses his wife's criticism of the gaoler in her petition. An erroneous impression had been created in her mind because she had not been allowed to visit him. It was from the cold that he suffered and not for want of sustenance:

> They do Mr Gittens injury who say that I have wanted either meat or drink competent since I was committed unto this custody. I am likelier to starve for cold than for want of meat. My wife, indeed, cannot be permitted to come unto me: she knoweth not how I fare—and therefore, she may be in fear that I am, in regard of meat and drink, hardlier used than I am or have been.

The preliminary examinations were conducted before justice Young and Dr Vaughan and his brother, and it was at this time that Penry wrote his *Declaration of Faith and Allegiance.* The public examinations took place in the Old Bailey before magistrates on 5 April 1593 when he was remanded. Five days later, on 10 April, he was again examined before Henry Fanshawe and Richard Young. One of the questions put to him at this examination related to his refusal, as a man of scholarship and ability, to accept office in the Separatist Church in London. Penry's explanation was that he wished to be free from the constraints of office to labour for Wales, to secure the Gospel for his own countrymen. This was also his alleged reason for leaving his refuge in Scotland.

Following this examination he was returned to the Poultry Compter, where he wrote to the Separatists beseeching their prayers on his behalf. If they were banished they should leave the country as a body; the flock had to be kept together, and seek a land where they would be at liberty to worship as they desired. It would be advisable to reconnoitre the New Jerusalem beforehand and make preparations for the arrival of the others. He further expressed the hope that they would not be unmindful of his own family:

> Yea, I would wish you and them to be together, if you may, whithersoever you shall be banished, and to this purpose to

bethink you beforehand where to be; yea, to send some who may be meet to prepare you some resting place: and be all of you assured that He, who is your God in England, will be your God in any land under the whole heaven.

Penry's advice to the Separatists was timely, since Parliament was then discussing a measure to compel those who were unwilling to conform to the discipline of the Established Church, to leave for other havens; if they chose to remain the penalty would be death by hanging. In 1593 the Separatists, though their leaders, Henry Barrowe and John Greenwood, had already been hanged at Tyburn, were released from gaol, and departed for the Low Countries from where, in 1620, the Mayflower was to leave Leyden for New England in America.

John Penry's first appearance before Lord Chief Justice Popham at the King's Bench took place on 21 May. His books, and his private papers written while he was in Scotland, were produced in evidence against him. The papers were incriminating because they contained statements which could be interpreted as being in contempt of the Queen. He was indicted on two counts: first, of inciting sedition in the country and, secondly, of treasonable behaviour against the Head of the state church, the Queen herself. Penry was returned to prison.

Appreciating that the letters could be misconstrued, Penry now made a frantic appeal to the Queen's most trusted adviser, Lord Burghley, whom he must have known. He emphasised that the papers seized had been of a private nature, any statements in them which appeared derogatory of the Queen were the opinions of others and not his own. He had always been steadfast in his loyalty to his sovereign; his only desire had been to introduce the Gospel into his native land and to spread light where hitherto there had only been darkness. He further claimed that he was the first to labour to sow the seed:

I am a poor young man born and bred in the mountains of Wales. I am the first, since the last springing up of the Gospel in this latter age, that publicly laboured to have the blessed seed thereof sown in those barren mountains. I have often rejoiced before my God, as he knoweth, that I had the favour to be born and live under her Majesty, for the promoting this work. In the earnest desire I had to see the Gospel planted in my native country, and the contrary corruptions removed, I might well ... forget mine own danger: but my loyalty to my Prince did I never forget. And now being to end my days before I am come to the one half of my years, in the likely course of nature, I leave the success of these my labours unto such of my Countrymen as the Lord is to raise up after me, for the accomplishing of that work, which, in the calling of my country unto the knowledge of Christ's blessed Gospel, I began.

Penry was granted an interview with Cecil, and from another letter written to him a few days later it becomes clear that the great man had advised Penry to throw himself on the Queen's mercy. He wanted to follow Cecil's advice, but was prevented from doing so by a lack of pen and ink.

Penry's final appearance before the King's Bench took place on 25 May, with Chief Justice Popham presiding, when he was indicted of treason under the terms of the Act of Uniformity 1559. Predictably, he was found guilty and sentenced to be hanged. He was taken from the court to King's Bench prison to await execution. Penry did not have to linger long in chains for on Tuesday, 29 May, at 5 p.m., while he was sitting down to a meal, these were removed and he was dragged on a hurdle through the narrow filthy streets of the City to St Thomas a Watering, a place of execution by the river Thames, near the present Old Kent Road, where he was publicly hanged. He was only thirty years old. So summary were proceedings that there were few people present to watch the last agonising moments. There were no crowds to scoff and jeer; no family or friends to bemoan his passing. It was in this ignominious fashion that a true son of Wales departed this vale of tears.

Penry's direct influence upon Wales was negligible. It is true that he was the first Puritan prophet to evangelise there, but he was an itinerant for about a year only, and he did not leave behind him a body of disciples; his was a lonely voice. Though between 1587-9 he published three notable volumes on religious conditions in the country of his birth, it is extremely doubtful whether they made any impact at all. Protestantism, let alone Puritanism, was making very slow progress in Wales, and since the books were written in English, they would have been incomprehensible to a largely monoglot Welsh population. Furthermore, quick action by the authorities meant that many copies were seized before they got into the hands of the populace. Neither were the clergy and gentry won over to his views and George Owen, the squire of Henllys in Pembrokeshire—and his views may well have been typical of those held by members of his class—described Penry 'as a shameless man'. It is certain that Penry had patrons who were far more distinguished that George Owen. Amongst them were Robert Dudley, Earl of Leicester, Elizabeth's favourite, William Cecil, Lord Treasurer and Principal Secretary, and Robert Devereux, the second Earl of Essex, and another who was much in favour with the Queen. But they all proved to be fair-weather friends, and they were to abandon Penry in his hour of need.

Following his execution in 1593, Penry became largely forgotten during the next two centuries, and was only re-discovered during the latter half of the nineteenth century, when to dissenting historians and publicists he became the 'morning star of Protestant Nonconformity in Wales'. The reasons for his long stay in the shadows are not difficult to discover. During his comparatively short working life of some seven years he influenced none in Wales and only a handful in London. Wales was not ready to receive his heady ideas, and his radicalism—towards the end of his career he was to join the religious Bolsheviks of the age, the Separatists—was deeply offensive to the higher authorities in church and state. He was a political incendiary, and as such had to be got rid of as soon as possible. Though today his trial would be regarded as a travesty of justice, it was viewed in an entirely different light in the sixteenth century. Then it was a case of an intensely disloyal subject receiving his just reward. It would have taken a very brave man indeed to have protested against the injustice of his treatment and execution.

A view that is widely held today is that it was Penry's patriotism, his passionate love of Wales, that drove him to vilify the bishops, convocation and the clergy, in other words the whole church establishment, in such unmeasured terms. However, the *Aequity*, the *Exhortation* and the *Supplication* can be regarded as essential components of a concerted propaganda campaign conducted by the Presbyterians to influence Parliament to effect reforms. Penry was an essential cog in the machine, because as a Welsh Puritan he could provide invaluable information about the failings of the church in his own country. Penry's primary concern was not about the state of religion in Wales; what was nearest and dearest to his heart was the triumph of Puritanism everywhere. His patriotism was a secondary consideration. Though his native heath saw very little of him he, nevertheless, enjoys a secure niche in the history of Wales for his intellectual courage, his championship of freedom of conscience and his genuine affection for the country of his birth.

NOTES

[1] The true faith still walks the land
That you loved beyond all others;
The lamp shines bright in ailing Bethel,
And clear rings the bell in many a church.
[2] Trevelyan, G.M., *History of England: The Illustrated Edition*, p. 326.
[3] These were the followers of Richard Cox and were representative of the moderate Puritans.
[4] These were the followers of John Knox and were extreme in their views.
[5] It was not until 1872 that the first university college was established at Aberystwyth.
[6] Salesbury possessed certain peculiarities as a translator. He was a Renaissance scholar and he deliberately latinised his vocubulary in order to demonstrate the Latin origin of words. Thus 'eglwys' (church) is derived from the Latin, 'ecclesia'. He wrote it as 'eccles'. He further omitted the mutation of consonants. 'Fy nhad' (my father) was written as 'vy tat'.
[7] Professor J.E. Neale argues that the literary evidence seems to point to Job Throkmorton as being Martin. Id., *Elizabeth and her Parliaments, 1584-1603*, p. 220.

COLONEL JENKIN JONES (1623-?)

Charles I, King of England, unfurled his standard at Nottingham on 22 August 1642 and the first Civil War had begun. By coincidence or design, this was the very day and month on which an ancestor of his, Henry Tudor, had raised his Red Dragon on Bosworth Field in 1485 when the Yorkist Richard III was defeated and slain.

Charles Stuart, like Henry, had sure grounds for assuming that he had the support of the vast majority of the Welsh people. The loyalty of the Welsh gentry—and their tenants would naturally follow their lead—to the Tudors was, in 1603, transferred to the Stuarts. However, in the process of change, this attachment had undergone a subtle transfiguration, since it now embraced not only the Crown itself, but also the whole complex of institutions through which the monarch governed, namely, Parliament, the law and the church establishment. It was for this reason that the loyalty of the Welsh was to survive the neglect and misrule which characterised Charles's reign. Support for an arbitrary despotism was no part of their creed, but any sympathies which they might have entertained for the parliamentary cause were soon swept away by the growing violence of the opposition to the King and particularly by its attack on the church.

But though the Welsh generally were to demonstrate their attachment to the Crown, there were within every shire in Wales pockets of parliamentary supporters. In certain limited areas, those which had commercial contacts with London or Bristol, or which had felt the influence of border Puritanism, they even predominated. Broadly speaking, Parliament drew its support from a minority among the gentry, and from the ranks of merchants, tradesmen, artisans and shopkeepers, the middle sort of men, and since Wales was economically backward compared with England, this middle-class element tended to be rather thin on the ground there.

A preponderance of the gentry of Breconshire drew sword for the King. However, there was a minority of disaffected among

Llanddeti Church

them who upheld the sovereignty of Parliament. Prominent among local opponents of the King were Sir William Lewis of Llangorse, Henry Watkins of Caebalfa, William Watkins of Pen-yr-Wrlodd, and Jenkin Jones of Llanddeti. These did not belong to old, well-established county families; rather were they new men motivated either by their Puritanism, or by business associations, or a combination of both.

Jenkin Jones was born in 1623 at Tŷ Mawr in the parish of Llanddeti. He was the son of a substantial landowner, John Jones or John ap John Howell, who died in 1646. Jenkins's eldest brother, while never achieving his eminence, nevertheless became sheriff of Breconshire in 1658. Academically, Jenkin Jones must have shown promise, for it is recorded that he matriculated at Jesus College, Oxford, in 1639. His unswerving loyalty to Parliament undoubtedly stemmed from his Puritanism and his Puritan connections. He had married as his second wife Barbara, the daughter of Sir Anthony Mansell of Briton Ferry, and the niece of Bussy Mansell. Bussy had defected to the parliamentary party, and rose to become a captain in the parliamentary army and a pillar of the cause in Glamorgan. Jenkin Jones was a notable Puritan preacher as well as being a soldier, and he delivered fiery sermons from his pulpit. He was, undoubtedly, the greatest Puritan personality in the county of Brecknock. A close associate of his was Vavasor Powell, the great apostle of the Puritans in Breconshire, who was a fellow student at Jesus College and who probably effected his conversion. However, despite his close friendship with Powell, there is little evidence that he agreed with the latter's sanguine views regarding the Second Coming of Christ or with his political outlook. After the outbreak of hostilities, Jenkin Jones soon came to the forefront as a soldier, and his zeal for the parliamentary cause was such that he raised, equipped and maintained, at his own expense, a troop of 120 horse from his relations, dependants and tenants. With their assistance he was able to keep the royalists in Breconshire in complete subjection. His loyalty to Cromwell, despite the fact that for a time he had been a thorough-going opponent of the Protectorate as a political innovation,[1] was demonstrated in March 1655, at the time of the Penruddock royalist uprising in Wiltshire, when he offered to serve the Protector with the 'good people of Breconshire'.

Following the defeat and execution of Charles I, such was the concern of the Commonwealth authorities at the slow spread of the Puritan gospel in the darker places of Wales that, in February 1650, an *Act for the Better Propagation and Preaching of the Gospel in Wales* was passed by Parliament. By this measure, which was to be in force for three years, authority in Wales was delegated to seventy-one commissioners, twenty-eight representing the shires of north Wales and forty-three those of the south. The majority of the commissioners were gentry, or prosperous yeomen and lawyers drawn from the more anglicised areas of the country. Naturally, they were all active parliamentarians and some were uncompromisingly Puritan in their attitudes. The vast majority had some experience in administrative or military posts.

Any five of these commissioners, acting together, could examine ministers and, if they thought fit, eject them from their livings. In 1650 one of those removed was Lewis Aubrey, the incumbent of Llanddeti. In this instance the living remained vacant until 1657. To avoid too many embarrassments of this nature a body of twenty-five 'Approvers' was established to select 'Godly and painful men, of approved conversation . . . to preach the Gospel in Welsh'. Any five of these could 'approve' ministers at a stipend of £100 per annum, the money to be obtained from the sequestered revenues of the church. Such was Jenkin Jones's known staunchness to the parliamentary cause, and the fervency of his Puritanism, that he was appointed one of the 'Approvers'. In this capacity he was involved, early in 1653, in an angry exchange of letters with three ejected clergymen, Thomas Lewis of Llanfeugan, Thomas Powel of Cantref and Griffith Hattley of Aberyscir. The three ministers wanted permission from Jenkin Jones to preach the gospel openly and freely 'among those that do much want it, and do as earnestly call for it as the parched earth after the dew and rain of Heaven'. They were very conscious of the fate that had befallen their fellow ministers in the previous spring, when some had been imprisoned, and others dragged from their pulpits for preaching abroad. The tenor of Jenkin Jones's reply left them in no doubt about the dire consequences were they to be so bold or foolish as to embark on what they proposed.

Together with his role as an 'Approver', Jenkin Jones also promoted the spread of the Puritan gospel by his acivities as an itinerant preacher, for which he received payment from the government. Though most of his time was spent in the Merthyr district, he was active also in north Glamorgan and the vale of Neath. Occasionally, he preached as far east as Llantilio Crossenny, not far from Monmouth. His activities as an itinerant placed him in considerable danger at times. In the parish of Aberystruth in Monmouthshire he was waylaid by one John James Watkins, a former Royalist soldier, whose expressed intention was to murder him.

The Propagation Act lapsed in March 1653 and the place of the commissioners was taken in 1654 by a body known as the Triers, composed of nine laymen and twenty-nine ministers operating from London. These Triers were godly, moderate men with high standards. The system of itinerant ministers, which had been promoted by the commissioners to remedy the 'famine of the word' caused by the dearth of suitable ministers, was now abandoned. In future, ministers were to be licensed only if they had been provided with a testimonial signed by at least three responsible persons, including a settled minister. One of those who received the blessing of the Triers was Jenkin Jones, and by 1657 he appears to have been admitted as a minister in his home parish of Llanddeti, appropriating for his own use the rectory, glebe and church.[2] The three 'sober Christians' who signed his certificate were Rice Williams of Newport, Wroth Rogers of Hereford, and Robert Weaver of Radnor.

As a minister, he shared much in common with the Baptists. He certainly agreed with them that baptism should be by complete immersion, and that adults only should be baptised. On the other hand, he could not accept the other exclusionist idea held by John Miles who, in 1649, had established a Baptist church at Ilston in Gower, that only Particular Baptists should be admitted to the Lord's table. He was prepared to admit members of all the sects to the ordinance of communion. According to Dr Calamy, Jenkin Jones was a Catabaptist, and his ideas concerning free communion were broadly similar to those held by the Quakers.

However, Jenkin Jones's activities as an itinerant and as a settled minister did not diminish his interest in the real world around him, and his sword always remained conveniently close to his hand. His zeal for the Commonwealth meant that he retained his interest in politics, and he became particularly involved with municipal matters in Brecon, the county town. Since the borough had the right to return a member to the Parliament at Westminster, control of the levers of power within the corporation was a matter of decisive importance. At Michaelmas 1659 (29 September) a dispute occurred over the election of the bailiff, the returning officer for parliamentary elections, and other officers of Brecon. What little information is available about the quarrel is contained in a tract entitled, *An Alarum to Corporations*, which professed to expose the 'unjust, barbarous, inhumane, traitorous practices of some of the Anabaptists' in opposing the election of one William Thomas to the office of bailiff. Unfortunately, the tract is fiercely partisan and could well have been written by William Thomas himself. In 1652 he had been a prime mover of the petition against the Propagators and he had continued to sustain his attacks on them. These attacks, naturally enough, had not endeared him to Jenkin Jones, and the Tract relates how Jones, and a leading member of his congregation at Llanddeti, Captain John Morgan,[3] had used force of arms to coerce the burgesses to support their candidate, John Lewis.[4] They were even accused of seeking to 'erect a righteous government, after the mode of John of Leyden[5] and Knipperdolling.[6] The upshot was that both candidates were elected. The matter could not be allowed to rest there, and so the governor of Hereford and Jenkin Jones, hardly impartial adjudicators, were called upon to arbitrate. They found both elections to be irregular, and advised that one Henry Powell should be appointed bailiff. According to the author of the tract what happened at Brecon was a clear warning to other corporations, and even to the City of London itself, as to what could befall them under the rule of the Puritans. It is hardly surprising that, under the Protectorate, such attempts should have been made at remodelling the corporations. The times were revolutionary and disturbed, and it was imperative that the government at Westminster should rivet its authority over the localities, by force if need be. Furthermore, it was desirable that the boroughs should return to the Parliament members of the right complexion, burgesses who were favourably disposed towards Oliver Cromwell, the Lord Protector.

Successive attempts at governing the country between 1649-1660 without a King, a House of Lords, and an established church having proved abortive, in 1660 the monarchy, amid the general acclamation of the people, was restored in the person of Charles II. This event was anathema to Jenkin Jones and the story is related of how, on being informed that Charles had landed, he mounted his horse and, riding through the churchyard, discharged his pistol at the priest's door exclaiming with great bitterness: 'Ah, thou old whore of Babylon, thou'lt have it

The door at Llanddeti at which Jenkin Jones discharged his pistol

all thy own way now'. The tale is possibly true since the door is pierced through, and the damage could have been caused by a ball discharged in this fashion. Further corroboration can be adduced from the fact that in 1878 a ball was found in some wall plaster removed from the chancel during repairs. It is now kept in Brecon Museum.

1660 witnessed the restoration of the monarchy, the House of Lords and the Established Church; the Cavaliers who had suffered so heavily in social and material terms during the Civil Wars and Commonwealth for their loyalty to the Crown, also came back and assumed what they considered to be their rightful place in society. The day of the 'usurper' had come to an end. For Jenkin Jones, the great nonconformist, there was little hope. He was evicted from his living of Llanddeti, where he was replaced by one John Morgan; his estates were confiscated and passed into the hands of Edward Hughes, a Brecon lawyer; and Jones found himself incarcerated, to the accompaniment of stone-throwing and derisive shouts, in Carmarthen gaol. His imprisonment arose from the fact that he and his friends would not 'forego their meetings'. Following his release on Sunday, 22 July 1660, Jenkin Jones returned to Llanddeti where he preached in the open air to a congregation estimated at between 500 to 600 drawn from Breconshire, Glamorgan, Radnor and Monmouth. He was said to have urged the people to fall upon the soldiers present who, to the number of about a dozen, together with three officers, had been sent to disperse the meeting by two magistrates, James Watkins and Henry Williams. Henry Williams, in a report of the incident to the authorities in London, declared that the design of the preacher and his followers was the overthrow of the new government. Jenkin Jones's servant was even overheard to say that the republicans would be even with the royalists within a week. Another of Jones's henchmen at the meeting, Captain John Morgan, a tailor by profession, and a sequestrator of church property in the county, was fined £200 for his part in the riot. The heaviness of the penalty was based on the assumption 'that his old post had not left him penniless'.

After spending a month in gaol Jenkin Jones was released, but intelligence that he was gathering followers together and delivering inflammatory speeches led, inevitably, to his being placed in prison again. He must have died shortly after this, for following this second incarceration, Jenkin Jones disappears from the pages of history though not without leaving a footprint in the sand. [7]

NOTES

[1] In protest he had signed the *Word for God* and, according to some of his enemies, even went as far as to gather soldiers together to fight against the new powers.

[2] Lambeth Augmentation Books.

[3] Infra, p. 63

[4] This was somewhat reminiscent of Pride's Purge. In December 1648 Colonel Pride and his musketeers excluded some 100 members from the House of Commons and imprisoned nearly 50 others.

[5] He was a well-known Anabaptist who had established an extraordinary regime in Münster in 1534-5. It became notorious for its extreme ideas like legalising bigamy. John of Leyden himself had sixteen wives.

[6] Bernard Knipperdollinck (1490-1536). He was a German Anabaptist and martyr.

[7] A Jenkin Jones resided at Kilgerran, near Cardigan in 1672 and licensed his house there as a Congregational place of worship. Thomas Rees was of the opinion that he was probably the Jenkin Jones of Llanddeti (*History of Protestant Nonconformity in Wales*, London, 1833). This assumption has to be unreservedly abandoned as the Kilgerran captain was a Pembrokeshire man, born and bred.

HOWELL HARRIS (1714-1773)

The eighteenth century bore witness to a great awakening within the Established Church by young spirits disillusioned with its deficiencies, and in the process they created a church within a church (*ecclesiola in ecclesia*). The weaknesses which the Hanoverian church failed to address were many and varied. There was the problem of English bishops being appointed to Welsh dioceses for political reasons, and since the four Welsh sees were amongst the poorest in the Kingdom, translations to richer sees in England were frequent. The unattractiveness of the Welsh bishoprics because of their poverty and remoteness, with their episcopal palaces often in a state of dilapidation, together with the political role of the bishops as members of the House of Lords which necessitated their attendance in London, meant that there was little inducement for them to visit their sees. Consequently absenteeism, common enough in previous centuries, was considerably accentuated. This non-residence led to a great neglect of pastoral duties, and candidates for the ministry were either left unconfirmed or were compelled to cross the border to be confirmed by a bishop in England. The twin evils of simony (offering financial inducements to gain preferment) and nepotism (conferring livings on relatives) were still only too evident and bishops, in order to augment their incomes, held livings *in commendam* (in addition to their bishoprics); the duties, in their absence, being performed by poorly paid curates.

Between these English-speaking Whig bishops and the lower clergy, who were predominantly Welsh in speech and recruited from the ranks of native society, there existed an unbridgeable divide. The lower clergy, also, were guilty of pluralism (holding more than one living at the same time) and absenteeism, and far too often the incumbents of Welsh parishes were monoglot Englishmen. As the eighteenth century progressed the number of graduate clergy began to decline, and it naturally followed that their standard of education also fell. The root cause of the problem was undoubtedly the poverty of the church, and this situation had arisen because of the impropriation of tithes by laymen who, in turn, paid miserable stipends to the vicars whom they appointed. The unbeneficed clergy, the curates, were even worse off, and seldom did they receive more than £10 a year. In consequence, to make both ends meet, they had to minister to several churches which could be miles apart. Very often, parishioners had to sit patiently in their cold, damp churches for hours awaiting the arrival on horseback of the curate, who might very well hurry through the service so that he could proceed elsewhere as soon as possible. The curates were usually very badly educated, and barely distinguishable from their parishioners, whom they would sometimes join after the service for a glass of ale. It is hardly surprising that they were accused of apathy and laxity. However, despite the defects in the church, it would be quite wrong to overdraw the picture, since there were within the church elements which were wideawake, zealous and reforming. The church was somnolent but it was certainly not beyond redemption.

The condition of post-Restoration society in which this church operated, in both England and Wales, was abysmal, and there were sincere people who were appalled by the vice, profanity, drunkenness and desecration of the Sabbath which were characteristic of the age. In London and elsewhere, societies were formed for the 'reformation of manners' (conduct) and through penal action initially it was hoped to bring about an improvement. There was a similar movement taking place in Germany known as the Pietist movement, and under the influence of these Pietists the London reformers came to the conclusion that prosecution in the courts alone would not achieve the desired end; it would have to be supported by some form of religious education. As a result, under the auspices of the S.P.C.K.,[1] charity schools sprang up like mushrooms with the avowed purpose of imparting education so that souls might be saved, and some ninety-six were established in Wales by 1737. To add to the ferment of opinion, Moravian missionaries from their religious community at Herrnhut, in Saxony, now appeared in London. They believed that personal piety and good works were not enough; each individual had to become conscious of sin and experience personal salvation. And at Oxford, in 1729, quite independently of the Moravians, John Wesley, one of the founders of Methodism in England, had established the 'Holy Club'. The soil had also been prepared by the Dissenters and the Circulating Schools of Griffith Jones of Llanddowror. The Methodists were actively supported by Dissenting ministers, and it is significant that early Methodism flourished where Dissent was strongest. It was a case, indeed, of rekindling fires on warm hearths. As for the Circulating Schools, their appearance signified the appearance of a new dawn since the advance in literacy went hand in hand with the development of Methodism. It is against this background, also, of a growing awareness of the need to reform society, and to save souls, that the Methodist Revival in Wales, together with its central figure, Howell Harris, have to be considered.

Howell Harris was born on 23 January 1714 at Trefeca-fawr, the son of a farmer, Howell Powell, alias Harris, and his wife Susannah Powell of Trefeca-fach. Harris's father had moved from Llangadock, Carmarthenshire, to Talgarth *c.* 1700 and soon after his arrival there, in 1702, he had married Susannah. They had three sons, Howell being the youngest. His two elder brothers, Joseph and Thomas, sought to make their fortunes in London, the Mecca of all ambitious Welshmen. Both were to achieve success, Joseph in the Mint, and Thomas as a master tailor. Howell was destined for a career in the church, and to equip himself for the task, he took advantage of what educational opportunities there were available locally. He entered Llwyn-llwyd, a dissenting academy, but his prospects were blighted by the death of his father when he was only eighteen years old. He now opened a school at Llangorse, and he was a schoolmaster there from 1732-5. These were 'wild and giddy' days, but when he was twenty-one, all this was to change, and in a sensational fashion. On Palm Sunday 1735, he was deeply moved by a sermon delivered by the vicar of Talgarth, Pryce Davies, which led him to attempt to mend his ways. On the homeward journey, as he reflected on the clergyman's words, he decided to put his resolution to the test by effecting a reconciliation with a neigh-bour with whom he had been at variance. On the following Whitsunday, after weeks of mental anguish, he experienced conversion which brought him the peace of mind which he so greatly desired. Having found deliverance, and received assurance of forgiveness and the remission of sins, he decided to secure these blessings for others, and despite the opposition of his vicar, who shared in the general aversion of the times to any manifestation of 'enthusiasm', he began to evangelise in the vicinity of his home. The first permanent society (*seiat*) was established by him at *Y Wernos*, a farmhouse in Llandyfalle, in 1737. Others were then organised around Talgarth in the houses of people of quality. From Brecknockshire he moved into Radnorshire and Montgomeryshire and then, availing himself of the support of Dissenting ministers, into Monmouthshire and Glamorgan. He even crossed the border into England, such was his zeal for saving souls. Harris sincerely believed that he had been appointed God's agent to carry out the divine will here on earth, and though he was conscious of his own deficiencies for this great crusade—he was not an ordained minister—he plunged into the fray with a vigour which bordered on frenzy. For him life became a mission to fight Satan and the forces of darkness, and he was to become the principal ark-bearer of the Methodist cause. He still aspired to Holy Orders, and as a step towards the realisation of this goal, he matriculated in November 1735 at St Mary Hall, Oxford. His friends were delighted at the prospect of Harris pursuing a university career as they hoped that a period at university would 'cure him of his fanaticism'. However, it was not to be, and within a week he had left Oxford never to return. A considerable sacrifice was involved in this decision to leave the university, for a local gentleman had promised him the headship of a grammar school, together with an incumbency which would have brought him an additional salary of £140 per annum, were he to finish the course. Harris now applied for Holy Orders, but was refused on the grounds that he was preaching irregularly, and doubtless his own vicar had a great deal to do with the decision. He was to apply for ordination on three subsequent occasions, but Nicholas Claggett, the bishop of St David's, was to refuse them all. Harris now consulted his mentor, Griffith Jones, later to be dubbed the

'Methodist Pope', at Llanddowror as to what he should do next. He knew Jones well as he visited Llanddowror regularly, and such was the relationship between the two men that, for a short time, he was to act as superintendent to Griffith Jones's Circulating Schools. The older man counselled moderation, and advised Harris to study to prepare himself for the ministry. This advice Harris rejected as he felt that he could achieve more by exhorting than by reading. Jones now called him 'a railer, proud and haughty' but despite this furious outburst—Harris always lived in dread of Jones's sharp tongue—he was still determined to carry on with his mission.

Whatever this mission was—apart from the saving of souls, there was great uncertainty about its nature—Harris was adamant that it was not to lead people out of the Established Church, an institution which he greatly revered. Despite the confusion about aims, and Harris was to inform George Whitefield, one of the great leaders of Methodism in England,[2] that 'we are like little children not knowing what to do', he wished to remain within the church; he would have no truck with secession. His desire was to revive the church, not destroy it. His position is demonstrated by his reluctance to accept communion from the hands of Dissenting ministers, for he believed that only ordained clergy could administer the sacraments, though ordination was not required for preaching. On the other hand he did have considerable sympathy with those who were reluctant to take communion at the hands of unworthy priests. Harris, furthermore, had no quarrel with bishops, and he was always at pains to hold meetings at times which would not conflict with church services. It was, undoubtedly, as a result of his influence that the first Association meeting at Dygoedydd, near Llandovery, in January 1742, declared that the movement would not 'go out of the church till turned out'. This decision to remain within the church brought to an end the early co-operation with the Dissenters. Arrogantly, he accused them of aridness and lukewarmness, and his strictures caused a great deal of ill-feeling though, eventually, he and the older Nonconformists were to be reconciled.

BRECONSHIRE'S METHODIST CONNECTIONS

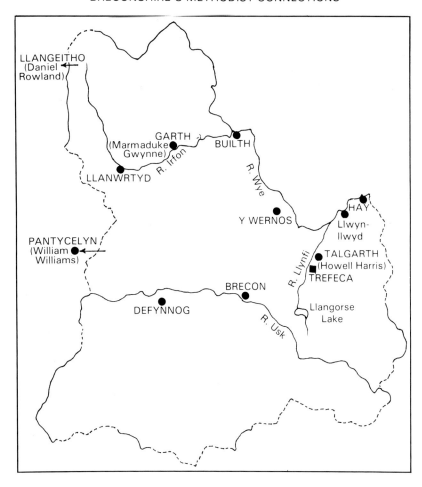

Harris's role in the Methodist movement was twofold: first, as an impassioned, fiery free-lance evangelist; and secondly, as an extremely gifted organiser. *Ffydd yn y galon yn hytrach na synnwyr yn y pen*[3] sums up admirably the attitude of the Methodist preacher and, apart from Daniel Rowland, Harris was as fine an exponent of this type of appeal as any of the other leaders. He overwhelmed his hearers by the sheer force of his personality and thunderous voice. They would be strangely moved, and in their 'enthusiasm' would indulge in the most extraordinary behaviour. Some would weep, quake, tremble, or clap their hands, while others would cry as if in agony, or swoon and fall prostrate to the ground. It was highly emotional scenes like these that won for the Methodists the name of 'jumpers' and brought the movement into disrepute. When Harris was in full flight he would sweat profusely, and occasionally vomit. He would often preach *extempore*, the theme being suggested 'where the Book opened', and the ensuing sermon could last for up to four hours, a considerable feat of stamina in itself. Although he always maintained that he did not preach, only exhorted—the inspired amateur—he, nevertheless, attracted large crowds and he was to claim, though he doubtless exaggerated, that he addressed audiences of between 10,000-12,000, a number that could not have been accommodated in any church, or in any other building for that matter, so that he was constrained to preach out of doors. Doubtless, amongst his hearers were many who came to scoff but who remained to pray. Harris was quite happy to preach anywhere, on the mountainside, in fields, churchyards, fairs, wakes, revels, towns, barns, out-houses and meeting houses. Any place would suffice, and in 1737 he explained that he was prepared to meet people 'in the mud, or under a hedge, or in a pigsty'. Later, the societies built chapels for themselves; one of the earliest in Wales, as indicated by the name, being Alpha chapel in Builth. Harris was the one who initiated field preaching and, riding on horseback, he would often travel 150 miles a week and preach twice or oftener each day on as little as four hours sleep. He estimated that during a lifetime of itinerancy he had travelled altogether 80,000 miles. Writing to a friend regarding a journey he had made in north Wales, he said: 'I was seven nights in succession during this journey without undressing, and travelled a hundred miles from the morning of one day to the evening of another, without having any rest, preaching at midnight or in the early morning on the mountains'. The routine was extremely harsh and demanding, and Harris was called upon to operate in all kinds of weather, partake of all manner of food, and rest his weary bones on many an uncomfortable bed. Considering these hardships it is hardly surprising that he suffered from a variety of maladies including toothache, gout and haemorrhoids.

Harris, as a born again Christian, was determined to save 'poor illiterate souls chained in the dens of darkness'. The recurring theme in his sermons was hell and damnation, and a largely illiterate populace was to be cowed into mending its ways by harrowing tales of the fate that inevitably awaited those who had failed to win salvation. They would be consigned to the fires of hell, where they would suffer indescribable torments, and have their bodies rent asunder by fiends. Harris was to inform one sinner that 'unless God claims your heart, he will see the devils tearing your body and soul at the hour of death and on the day of judgement'. After all the gloom, and grim prophecies of impending doom, his hearers would not be left bereft of hope in a black pit of despair. They would be uplifted by promises of salvation, and the road to that blissful state was through repentance. However, the fire and brimstone approach gradually came to be softened, and the Methodists began to dwell less on the all-devouring and consuming flames of hell, and more on the soothing, saving balm of salvation. This new attitude was strikingly demonstrated by Harris at a public hanging in Haverfordwest in 1769 when he told the gaping throng: 'Thus did our Lord once hang on the Cross for you and me'.

Harris, like the other Methodist leaders, was subjected to considerable ill-treatment at the hands of clergy, gentry, magistrates and mobs. At times, and particularly when he was preaching in the towns, he went in fear of his life, and this persecution may well have helped his cause. He possibly endured more personal abuse than any of the other leaders, and they were to suffer enough. He was mobbed and in danger of his life at Swansea, Newport, Pontypool, Usk and Monmouth. At Crug-las, Swansea, a drunkard, egged on by Harris's enemies, aimed a pistol at him. The pistol misfired, and the would-be intoxicated assassin went to sleep on a lime-kiln, where he was overcome by fumes and died. Even the Duke of Beaufort became involved, and he led a mob which attacked Harris when he preached against drunkenness, society balls, whoredom and horse-racing. In north Wales, also, he had several narrow escapes, and at Bala, where local clergymen had plied the mob with drink to inflame it, he had concluded that it was 'his lot to die like Stephen in the midst of his enemies'. Nearer home he was denounced by the local clergy as a deceiver of the people, and Marmaduke Gwynne of Garth had gone to listen to him preach at Llanwrtyd churchyard with a copy of the Riot Act in his pocket fully intending to commit him as an incendiary. However, he ended up being led into the arms of Methodism. In 1744 the Grand Jury made a presentment against him at the Brecon Assizes, accusing him of attempting to subvert the established religion and undermine orderly government. His activities 'con-founded' the minds of his hearers, and brought together 'great numbers of disorderly Persons'. Four of his followers were pressed and placed in the town's gaol. Harris was to declare that in Breconshire and Carmarthenshire the Methodists were hunted 'like partridges'. He was repeatedly charged by the clergy and magistrates of contravening the Conventicle Act (1664),[4] a charge which he strenuously denied by declaring that he was a conformist and consequently not subject to the penalties of the statute. Harris, by the tone, manner and content of his sermons, easily aroused unfettered passions to which justices and constables alike only too often turned a blind eye. For him life in the front line was not easy or comfortable.

But though Harris alienated many, he also won converts, and in their ranks were two young men who were to become prominent in the movement. These were William Williams of Pantycelyn (1716-91) and Howell Davies (1716-70). William Williams was motivated to pursue a different path after hearing Harris preach in the churchyard at Talgarth in 1738. He described the experience in these words:

Dyma fore byth mi gofiaf
Clywais innau lais o'r Nef,
Daliwyd fi gan wŷs oddiuchod.
Gan ei sŵn dychrynllyd Ef.[5]

His ambition had been to become a doctor, an aspiration which he now abandoned in favour of the church. He took holy orders and became, for a time, a curate at Llanwrtyd where the vicar was Theophilus Evans, an unbending Anglican, and an implacable opponent of the Methodists. William Williams's contribution to the spread of Methodism was to be incalculable since he became the hymn writer of the movement, and about 1,000 of these lyrical masterpieces flowed from his pen, many composed by him while riding to one of his meetings. Howell Davies, who had an uncle living in Llanspyddid, near Brecon, was converted in the same year when he was a schoolmaster at Talgarth. He became a curate to Griffith Jones himself at Llandeilo Abercowin but, in 1741, he moved to Llys-y-frân, Pembrokeshire, where, for a time, he worked in a similar capacity. Jones was opposed to his itinerant activities, but Davies became a highly persuasive evangelist, and it was not without justification that he came to be dubbed the 'Apostle of Pembrokeshire'.

Together with being an impassioned orator, Harris also possessed considerable administrative gifts and in 1736 he began to organise his converts into societies (*seiadau*). Soon there were forty of these societies in Breconshire alone. He was to declare later that he had established the societies 'in imitation of the societies which Dr Woodward had given an account of in a little treatise on the subject'. Most of the society members were young, the majority being in their twenties and thirties. But as well as being youthful, a large number, particularly among the women, were unmarried. The presence of so many nubile, single women at society meetings inevitably placed temptations in the way of the exhorters and led to strains being imposed on married life. Harris himself was not impervious to the temptations of the flesh, and he certainly enjoyed the company of attractive, well-bred women. When he met Madam Bridget Bevan of Laugharne, wife of Arthur Bevan M.P., a lady of some beauty and charm, he found in the experience 'a taste of heaven'. Harris was often torn between his Christian beliefs and his sexual cravings. Young girls figured frequently in his dreams, and on occasions he was reluctant to go to bed, 'lest I should sin'. He was eventually to succumb to temptation and fall from grace. But the opportunities presented at society meetings for illicit liaisons provided the critics of Methodism with a glorious chance, which they eagerly seized, for indulging in mud-slinging, and their depiction of Methodist meeting places as dens of iniquity, where all kinds of carnal deeds were performed, gained some credence.

On average the number of people in a society numbered between ten and thirty. Meetings were held at least once a week, and until Methodist chapels were built, they were held in private houses or isolated farms. There was a weekly levy of 1*d*. to 2*d*., though poor members were excused. The conduct of affairs within a society was the province of the exhorter (*cynghorwr*) and he was assisted by stewards and catechisers; even private disputes lay within his domain. These exhorters were recruited mainly from the ranks of the artisans, though many of the rank and file members were minor gentry or prosperous farmers. Over the exhorters were set superintendents, and their areas of responsibility could embrace whole counties. While Wesleyan Methodism had developed along episcopal lines, the Welsh Calvinistic Methodists evolved a presbyterian organisation. In Wales the local societies sent representatives to a monthly meeting (*cwrdd misol*), over which was superimposed a quarterly meeting (*cwrdd cwarter*), the whole movement being controlled by the Association (*Sasiwn*). This was the policy-making body, and it also had the task of approving the exhorters. At the first Association meeting at Dygoedydd in 1742 Harris was appointed General Superintendent of the societies, though the clerical members would have preferred Daniel Rowland because he was an ordained clergyman. A potentially divisive and embarrassing situation was resolved by assigning to each his own sphere of operation, Harris in south-east Wales and Rowland in the south-west.

Methodism in Wales was to develop independently of the movement in England. Any link between them was provided by Harris, who established contact with both the English Methodist leaders, John Wesley and George Whitefield. Harris was always to endeavour to forge closer links between the various branches of Methodism, and between the Methodists and the Moravians.

Initially, he was a warm advocate of Wesley, whom he first met in 1739 at Bristol, a city which Harris visited frequently as there was a Welsh society there. He invited Wesley to come to Wales, and the Englishman was to visit the country on no fewer than forty-six occasions. Wesley was to find the Welsh language a real barrier, though it scarcely justified his conclusion that the Welsh were as ignorant as the Cherokee Indians. In 1746, at Neath, an accommodation was reached between the two men whereby they agreed not to proselytise 'each other's people' but to preach to them only by invitation, and Harris was invited by Welsey to attend his conferences, a signal honour. Because the language of Wesleyan Methodism was English, it did not become a significant factor in Welsh life until the nineteenth century. A cause was certainly established at Brecon, a town which was experiencing rapid anglicisation in the eighteenth century, for the borough was frequently visited by John Wesley and his brother Charles, the great hymn writer. In 1756 Wesley preached in the town hall, and his influence led to the formation of an English Wesleyan Society, which used to meet in private houses.[6] The need for a proper meeting house soon arose and, in 1770, a chapel was erected at the corner of Free Street and Little Free Street. It was from Brecon that the Rev. John Hughes, the son of a hatter, was dispatched on a mission to north Wales, where the first Wesleyan chapel was established at Denbigh in 1802.

Harris met Whitefield, the originator of the Methodist Movement in England, in March 1739, when he was taken by him to a Moravian meeting and came under their spell. In 1741 the ranks of the Methodists in England were split by a great controversy sparked off by theological differences, and the movement became divided between the Calvinism of Whitefield and the Arminianism of Wesley. Harris and the Welsh Methodists sympathised with Whitefield's theology, though Harris was never to become personally estranged from Wesley. Thus began the close association between the Welsh Calvinists and Whitefield's supporters in England known as 'Lady Huntingdon's Connexion'.[7] At the Association meeting held at the new Congregational chapel at Watford, near Caerphilly, in 1743, Whitefield was appointed Moderator, an act which signified a desire to maintain some link, however tenuous, between the two movements. This arrangement could work both ways, for Harris also deputised for Whitefield as Moderator, and it was in this capacity that Harris, when Whitefield left in 1739 on a mission to Oglethorpe's colony in Georgia in North America, became, for a time, a powerful force in English Methodism.

In 1750 it was the turn of the Welsh Methodists to be rent asunder, a situation which arose because of a quarrel between Harris and Rowland. At the best of times Harris was not an easy man to work with, since he was very imperious by nature. He was certainly not prepared to play second fiddle to Rowland, for he was obsessed with his own personal standing in the movement. He declared proudly that he 'had the honour of being sent out first to the fields'. Despite his own worthiness, he was extremely jealous of Rowland's gifts and influence. Furthermore, Harris possessed no sense of humour, and this contrasted sharply with Rowland's cheerfulness and zest for living. Apart from this clash of personalities, the influence which the Moravians exercised on Harris was a source of embarrassment to Rowland. Harris was considerably influenced by their doctrine of Patripassianism, which taught that God himself had died in Christ on the Cross, and the blood shed was God's blood. While Harris was offended by Rowland's occasional bouts of levity, Rowland was equally shocked and offended by Harris's lapses in personal morality. Harris's marriage on 18 June 1744 to Anne, the daughter of John Williams, the wealthy squire of Ysgrin ('Skreen'), Radnorshire, had been a mistake,[8] and though she occasionally itinerated with him, more often than not she stayed at home. In 1748 he met Madam Sidney Griffith, the attractive wife of the squire of Cefn-amwlch in Llŷn, and was completely swept off his feet, for he found in her qualities which were lacking in his own wife. Madam Griffith's marriage, also, was an unhappy one as her husband was a violent drunkard. Harris believed that she was possessed of prophetic powers, and she was invited to accompany him on his travels. Tongues inevitably began to wag, and there is little doubt that the relationship was an adulterous one. Madam Griffith's husband disowned her, while Harris and his wife became estranged. The much publicised affair reduced Rowland and the other leaders to despair and brought Methodism itself into disrepute. The simmering disagreements came to a head at the Association held at Llanidloes in May 1750, when the two leaders went their separate ways, and their people, thereafter, began to meet in separate associations. In July, at Llantrisant, Harris was expelled from the Association on the grounds of heresy and, deeply wounded, he withdrew to a self-imposed exile at Trefeca, despite the entreaties of Charles Wesley, who implored him not to retreat from the field with the battle not yet won. His cup of unhappiness overflowed in 1752 when two objects very dear to him were lost: his horse and his lover; the one he gave away, while the other died. The schism in the ranks of the Methodists had the effect of permanently weakening the movement in south-east Wales, and temporarily damaging it generally. It was not until 1762 that the leaders were reconciled, but the movement had been deprived of the services of one of its most stalwart members for some twelve crucial years. Though the wounds were healed in 1762, Harris was never to regain his old position within the movement; he was never again a prince. Though he attended Association meetings, visited societies, and preached, the former enthusiasm was missing—his failing health may have had something to do with it—and he was very conscious of the strong opposition of the unordained exhorters who refused to be guided by him any longer. Furthermore, the focus of his attention was now Trefeca. But there were occasions when the old flame burned fiercely again, and then he would become the target for ancient animosities. On one occasion, after preaching in a Welsh village, he was pursued by a furious mob who consigned both him and his gig to a ditch.

At his retreat in Trefeca Harris established a family from among his supporters, and in this design he was stoutly supported by Evan Moses, an Aberdare tailor, who recruited in the wake of his master all over Wales, and Thomas William of Eglwys Ilan. With the aid of a gift of £900 from Madam Griffith, he transformed the small farmhouse at Trefeca into a large castellated mansion in the neo-Gothic style which came to be dubbed 'the New Jerusalem' by his enemies. The *cartref* housed a community similar to those established by the Moravians at Herrnhut in Saxony and Fulneck in Yorkshire. The estate comprised 765 acres and offered employment in some sixty different crafts. In addition to farming, and experiments were conducted to increase the yield of crops such as wheat, barley, oats, turnips, beans and potatoes, and to produce sheep, cattle and pigs of better quality, skills such as wool-spinning, dyeing, weaving, building, road-surveying, wood-felling, shoemaking and tailoring were practised. By 1759 even a printing press had been introduced. Such was the reputation of the farmers and artisans at Trefeca that enquiries about securing their services were received from as far afield as Leominster and Bristol. Trefeca was a monastery, a farm and a labour colony, but it was also a reformatory, as carnal men and thieving women were sent there to have their ways mended. Harris was head of the 'family', and he imposed an authoritarian régime. Each member was obliged to address him as 'Father'. Those who joined, and there were about 120 members altogether, including men, women and children, came from all over Wales, some even from England, to 'fix their tents' there. They forfeited all their worldly goods and shared in the profits. The grounds were landscaped, and when John Wesley visited the community in August 1763, he found Harris's house

Trefeca

one of the most elegant places he had seen in Wales, and the gardens, orchards, and fish-ponds a little paradise. The regimen imposed by Harris was hard. The day's work began at 4 a.m., the food was plain, and religious services were held three times a day during the week and four times on Sunday. The result was that the weaker brethren defected. However, despite the rigours of life in the 'New Jerusalem', the demands of the Seven Years' War (1756-63), and the ravages of smallpox which claimed the lives of over eighty people, including in 1749 that of his 'loving, winning, sharp and amiable' two-year-old daughter, Anne, the community prospered.

Harris, though possessed of only modest intellectual gifts, was very receptive of new ideas; he was an innovator. In 1755 the Brecknockshire Agricultural Society was established by Charles Powell, the squire of Castell Madoc, an estate situated about six miles outside Brecon on the Epynt road. This society was the first of its kind to be established in Wales, and Harris became an honorary member in recognition of his generosity in paying the government bounty money, which he had received for the recruits he had raised, into the hands of the society treasurer. Many of the new ideas circulating amongst improving landlords, and Harris could count himself as one, were introduced at his settlement. The food produced by the 'family' was used not only to sustain them; it also helped to provide for the needs of a rapidly expanding population outside.

In 1768 the ailing Selina, Countess of Huntingdon, the 'Queen of the Methodists', doubtless encouraged by Harris, established an academy at Trefeca for the purpose of training young men for the ministry. To accomplish her design she leased Trefeca-isaf farmhouse from Joseph Harris because of its proximity to Howell's settlement. It was opened as a college 'for literary and religious instruction' on 24 August 1768, the anniversary of Lady Huntingdon's birthday, the preacher for the occasion being George Whitefield. The students, who numbered about twenty, were drawn from all parts of the country, and on Saturdays they would leave in large numbers, some on horseback, to preach. They were a carefully selected band of missionaries as only such

Trefeca College
Founded by Selina, Countess of Huntingdon

'as were truly converted to God, and resolved to dedicate themselves to His service', were allowed entry. Otherwise, admission
was not confined to Methodists; students from all Protestant
denominations, including the Anglican Church, could qualify.
Harris took a great interest in the work of the academy, and it was
his custom to address the students twice weekly, on Tuesdays and
Thursdays. The course lasted three years, the expenses involved
in educating, boarding and lodging the students being borne by
the Countess. She also clothed them, and each student was provided every year with a new suit of clothes together with two
pairs of boots. The curriculum was broad-based embracing
'Grammar, Logic, Rhetoric, Ecclesiastical history, Natural Philosophy, and Geography, with a great deal of practical divinity
and languages'.

   The danger of invasion from Catholic France in 1759, together
with the promptings of his brother, Joseph, from London, led
Harris to join the county militia formed for the defence of the
realm. He was quite intrepid in the face of danger, and it did not
matter to him whether he died naturally or by a French musket or
sword. Popery was not to triumph, and to him the war was a

crusade against Satan. However, he still insisted as a condition of his enrolment that he should be allowed to preach. The Methodists were not radicals; they were essentially conservative, and Harris found no difficulty in drinking the health of the sovereign. The state of men's souls was his main concern, and he preached obedience to the laws of the realm, even though they might be unjust and oppressive. The community at Trefeca was now entrusted to the care of Evan Moses, and from the community Harris recruited twenty-four men to follow him, twelve of whom he undertook to arm and clothe at his own expense. They were incorporated into the county militia early in 1760, Harris himself with the rank of ensign though he was soon to be promoted to captain. Another five men from the 'family' joined the 58th Regiment at Hereford and, in 1759, three were to fight for General Wolfe at Quebec. However, only one was to return to Trefeca. Harris and his men now proceeded to Yarmouth, passing on their way through Abergavenny, where he preached in the market place, and Bedford, where he discussed with the Moravians the possibility of union. Though in danger of his life from the mob, wearing his uniform, he preached at Yarmouth and established a society there. The following year, preaching at every town through which he passed, he returned to Brecon with his company. He spent the winter of 1760-1 at the town, during which time he evangelised extensively, and used his authority as captain to quell disturbances at his meetings. If he was not listened to in silence, he would draw his sword and place the naked blade on the table before him. He would then throw back his cloak to display his uniform, and demand attention in the name of the King. It was a ploy that he was to use very successfully on several occasions. The summer of 1761 found Harris and his men at Bideford in the West Country, where again he strove to bring the Methodists and the Moravians together. In 1763 peace was concluded between England and France, and Harris immediately relinquished his commission and returned to the bosom of his 'family' at Trefeca.

On 21 July 1773, when he was sixty years old, Howell Harris breathed his last. The long years of itinerant preaching, the relentless persecution, the bitter doctrinal quarrels, the constant outpouring of energy, had finally taken their toll, and in his last illness he was to suffer considerable pain. Death, however, had lost its sting for him, and he joyfully departed this life in the sure expectation of life eternal. Twenty thousand people attended his funeral, but at Talgarth parish church, where the service was to be conducted according to the rites of the Church of England, three clergymen in turn were overcome with emotion. It was in complete silence that the body was interred in the chancel, in the same grave as his wife, who had died earlier on 9 March 1770, aged fifty-eight.

Apart from a small apartment at Trefeca for the use of his daughter, Elizabeth, Harris left his entire property for the maintenance of his settlement at Trefeca. Elizabeth was to marry a Catholic, Charles Prichard of Brecon, a surgeon, who was to occupy the office of bailiff of the town on three occasions: 1776, 1787 and 1797. The strictness of her upbringing had made her recoil from the puritanism of her father, and she was to reject his views and herself display a leaning towards Roman Catholicism.

Harris has been described as the Luther[9] of Wales, the Elijah of the Principality. He appeared as a comet in the night sky leaving a long tail behind. His profile, with its jutting jaw and piercing eyes, reveals a strong personality, a man doggedly determined to achieve his goals. Though he was impetuous, abrasive, arrogant, and a social climber, there is another side to his character for he could be compassionate and quick to pity. Furthermore, there is no doubting his single-mindedness of purpose which was to save souls. His iron constitution made it possible for him to travel incessantly, a task which, at times, demanded considerable physical courage. Religiously and socially, he was a conservative, and he had no desire to change the established order in church and state. Schism was anathema to him, and he endeavoured at all times to heal the wounds between the Methodist factions, and between them and the Moravians. He stood for Christian unity, and he saw himself 'as a peacemaker or reconciler of the brethren . . . a difficult work though a glorious one'. Methodism he conceived of as a reforming movement which had sprung up within the Established Church itself. But

Harris, like other great men before and since, had his Achilles heel, and his besetting weakness was a fondness for attractive women of wealth and standing. Despite his strong moral code he could, and did, succumb to temptation: the citadel did fall, and in the process he was to display a marked insensitivity towards the feelings of his wife. However, his virtues far outweighed his vices, and his greatest achievement was to wake the people of Wales from their spiritual torpor and to give them a new purpose in life. Cross-grained he undoubtedly was but he can be regarded, with some justification, as one of the creators of modern Wales and possibly the greatest Welshman of his age.

Howell Harris

NOTES

[1] Society for the Promotion of Christian Knowledge.

[2] He was, undoubtedly, the greatest of the English Methodist preachers. Once, in Yorkshire, when he was preaching, two members of the congregation died of fright but, with the bodies before him, he still proceeded to warn the silent gathering of the wrath to come.

[3] Faith in the heart rather than reason in the head.

[4] By this act attendance at meetings for religious rites, other than those of the Established Church, was punished by imprisonment for the first and second offence, and transportation for the third.

[5] Glorious morning ne'r forgotten
When to me from Heaven above
Came the voice that held me spellbound
With the power of its love.

[6] Vide, Thomas, W.S.K., *Georgian and Victorian Brecon*, Llandysul, 1993.

[7] Lady Huntingdon was Whitefield's patroness.

[8] Her father, and other members of the family, had been bitterly opposed to the match, and Anne was threatened and cajoled but to no avail. A wealthy aunt even offered £1.500 on condition that she gave up her lover. However, the couple succeeded in overcoming all obstacles, and they were married at Ystrad-ffin in Carmarthenshire.

[9] Martin Luther (1483-1546). He was a German Protestant reformer and the founder of Lutheranism.

DR THOMAS COKE (1747-1814)

The history of Wesleyan Methodism in Brecknockshire is inextricably linked with the name of Thomas Coke. A founder of Methodism in England, John Wesley, first visited Wales in 1739, and he established the first English cause in Cardiff in 1743. But Wesleyan Methodism in Wales, from its very inception, had to contend with many problems, and the principal one, undoubtedly, was language. Wesley, and the early Wesleyan preachers, spoke only English, and made little impact on what was, after all, a mainly monoglot Welsh population. It was Dr Coke, even though he could only master a few words in Welsh himself, who appreciated the need to bring salvation to the Welsh people in their own tongue. Brecon was a fertile vineyard for Wesleyan missionaries as, during the eighteenth century, there was a growing English-speaking element within the town.

Dr Coke's influence, however, was to extend far beyond his native heath. In England he became a stout pillar of Wesleyan Methodism, and he visited Ireland frequently, encouraging Methodist missionaries there to preach in the Irish language. He also attempted to promote Methodism on the Continent, particularly in revolutionary France, which he regarded as a fruitful field. But his activities were not confined to the domestic scene; like a Colossus he bestrode two worlds, the old and the new, Europe and America. The whole world was his stage and he a consummate player thereon.

Thomas Coke was born on 9 September 1747, the son of Bartholomew Coke, a wealthy apothecary in Brecon, whose medical knowledge was in great demand. Indeed, among his patients were the Gwynnes of Garth, one of whom, Sarah, married Charles Wesley, the great hymnist.

> He knew the cause of every malady
> Were it cold or hot or moist or dry.

Bartholomew was the son of Edward Cooke of Llanhamlach described as 'gentleman'. It was he who dropped an 'o' in Cooke

Thomas Coke

thus transforming Cooke into Coke. Bartholomew interested himself in civic affairs, and so successful was he that he occupied the prestigious office of bailiff on two separate occasions: in 1737 and yet again in 1758. For many years he was an alderman, and in 1768 a justice of the peace. His wife, Ann(e), was the daughter of Thomas Phillips of Trostre, Cantref, near Brecon. It was a happy

union marred by a great domestic tragedy, and that was the death
in infancy of their children, Bartholomew and John. They feared
that age would deny them another child; a fear which was dis-
pelled, however, in 1747 when Anne presented her overjoyed
husband with another boy, Thomas, the future Thomas Coke.
On this child the doting parents, naturally enough, lavished great
love and affection.

Thomas Coke entered Christ College soon after the appointment of David Griffith as headteacher (1757). Nothing is known
about his school days, but it is possible that his criticism of public
schools contained in his 'Sermon upon Education', delivered in
Somerset in 1773, is based largely upon his own experiences at
Brecon. His main objection to public schools was that the classical authors, which the boys were expected to study, were
profane and morally corrupting. He hinted, also, that in these
schools, discipline was the product of fear and not based, as it
should have been, on mutual respect between pupils and teachers.

From Christ College he proceeded, on 6 April 1764, to Jesus
College, Oxford, as a gentleman-commoner. University life at
this time was characterised by a great deal of vice and immorality
and Thomas, at an impressionable age, was to taste of that deb-
auchery. For a while he was even attracted by Deism, which was
fashionable at the time. He found, however, that it was very
difficult to steel himself against the pricks of conscience. He
triumphed over these temptations, but his experiences contributed to making him a more earnest and thoughtful person by the
time he left the University. In 1768 he took his B.A., and a few
years later, in 1770, his M.A. He now decided to enter the church
and on Trinity Sunday, 1770, he was ordained deacon in Christ
Church Cathedral, Oxford, and on 23 August 1772 a priest at the
Episcopal Palace, Abergwili, outside Carmarthen. In 1775, with
no less a person than Lord North, the Prime Minister, as his
patron, he obtained a Doctorate in Civil Law.

Thomas Coke shared his father's interest in local government
and, on 24 September 1769, he was made a common councillor of
Brecon and a year later, at the age of twenty-three, he was elected
bailiff. When his term of office ended, he was created an alder-

man, a position which he relinquished in 1772 because of his continual absences from the town. He had, by now, been installed as
curate of South Petherton in Somerset, and his visits to Brecon,
consequently, had become increasingly rare. However, for many
years afterwards, he continued to pay his contribution towards
the cost of civic dinners.

At South Petherton Coke was to spend six rather turbulent
years, for he succeeded in antagonising many members of his
congregation through his outspokenness from the pulpit, and by
his eagerness to effect repairs to the church fabric at the expense
of the ratepayers. Through the writings of John Wesley and John
Fletcher, he now came under the influence of Methodism and, on
13 August 1776, he decided to ride over to Kingston St Mary, near
Taunton, in Somerset, to meet, face to face, Wesley himself.
Wesley encouraged him to return to his parish, and convert it into
a Methodist circuit but Coke's 'enthusiasm' only succeeded in
stirring up fresh trouble for himself there. On Easter Sunday
1777, to the accompaniment of a triumphal peal on the church
bells, he was dismissed from his post and driven from the parish.
When, a few years later, Coke re-visited Petherton as a Methodist
preacher, the same bells rang out again but on this occasion in
welcome. On Coke's departure from the church, Wesley was to
write, 'Dr Coke being dismissed from his curacy, has bid adieu to
his honourable name, and determined to cast in his lot with us'.

Coke was now approaching his thirtieth birthday. For the next
few years his name appears among the preachers active in the
London circuit where Dr Coke, dressed in cassock and gown,
could be seen preaching to thousands in the open air. He was soon
travelling much further afield, and his energy and ability were
such that he was able to relieve Wesley of much work by visiting
far-flung societies on his behalf and undertaking much of the
administrative work. The reception accorded him, at times, was
hostile, and at Ramsbury, Wiltshire, he was to receive a particularly chilly welcome. When Coke was preaching in the open
square there, the vicar ordered the fire engine to spray water over
both preacher and listeners. Coke, infuriated at this treatment,
prophesied that providence would soon require the water to be

used for another purpose. True enough, a fortnight later, a fire broke out in the town which destroyed nearly all the houses in the square. In 1782 Coke paid the first of many visits to Ireland when he presided over the Conference of Irish preachers. John Wesley's health had now begun to fail—after all he was eighty-one years old—and in 1784 Coke played his part in drawing up the 'Deed of Declaration' which was lodged in the Court of Chancery, by means of which a Conference of a hundred specified men became his legal successor with power to fill up its ranks as death diminished them. This body was to be known thereafter as the 'Legal Hundred'.

From 1784 Coke's horizons were considerably, and significantly, broadened. As far back as 1768 the first American Methodist societies had been established by Irish immigrants, one at Sam's Creek, near Baltimore, and the other at New York. Between then and the outbreak of the War of American Independence (1776-83), Methodist societies proliferated like mushrooms, especially in Virginia. The main impetus was provided by the arrival of Francis Asbury, a blacksmith from West Bromwich, who became one of the greatest of the American circuit-riders. Since Wesley wished it, the Methodist societies were dependent upon the services of ordained clergymen to administer the rites of baptism and the sacraments. But the war brought such an arrangement to an end, because the success of the colonists[1] in that struggle caused a wedge to be driven between the Wesleyan Methodists in America and the established church in England. The Anglican clergy in America, when the war broke out, had, naturally enough, supported the British cause. When the hostilities were over, they ceased to be welcome in America and returned to England. The scattered congregations in America were consequently plunged into deep crisis as they could no longer have the sacraments administered to them. The bishop of London—and America was included in his diocese—conveyed the impression to Wesley that he did not intend doing anything about the situation, and so Wesley decided to act. Early in the morning of 1 September 1784, at 6 Dighton Street, Bristol, without consulting Conference, he ordained Richard Whatcoat and Thomas Vasey as deacons. On the following day he ordained them presbyters and consecrated Thomas Coke superintendent of the Methodists in North America. Shortly afterwards, Coke, accompanied by Whatcoat and Vasey, set sail for New York and arrived there on 8 November to an enthusiastic and generous welcome. A similar greeting was to be accorded him wherever he went during an exhaustive official tour. At the first Conference held at Baltimore later in the year, when sixty of the eighty-one preachers then in the active ministry attended, he ordained Francis Asbury and consecrated him as fellow superintendent. Three years later, the two men allowed themselves to be called bishop. Wesley, shocked at what he perceived to be the arrogance displayed by Coke and Asbury, wrote furiously:

How can you, how dare you suffer yourself to be called Bishop! I shudder, I start, at the very thought! Men may call me a knave or a fool, a rascal, a scoundrel, and I am content; but they shall never by my consent call me Bishop! For my sake, for God's sake, for Christ's sake put an end to this!

His outburst had no effect. The American Methodists were not to be dictated to by an old man living thousands of miles away. In 1784 the Methodist Episcopal Church of America became completely separated from its parent body.

By his writings and activities Coke contributed greatly to the consolidation of Methodism in America. He appreciated the importance of learning, and devoted much attention to the education of the young. An early fruit of his labours was the establishment of Cokesbury College, a school for the sons of preachers. His perambulations in America involved him in journeys fraught with danger, and he experienced many a narrow escape. But as if these traumatic experiences were not enough, he now vigorously assailed the evils of slavery with which he had been brought into contact almost daily. This had the effect of generating a great deal of ill will towards him. However, he and Asbury were allowed an interview with George Washington, the 'Father of his Country', on the subject of slavery when, to their unfeigned delight, they discovered that he entertained views very similar to their own.

Following his return to England, Coke attempted to stimulate the interest of people in establishing missions abroad. He drew attention to the heathen condition of the peoples of India, Africa, rural Ireland and Wales, and north-west Scotland, and appealed for volunteers and subscribers. These activities earned for him a rebuke from Wesley for his impractical idealism. In 1786 Coke returned to America with three preachers. At sea, the intrepid traveller encountered a violent storm caused, according to the captain, by the 'Methodist Jonah' on board. The fearful crew threw his sermons, and were sorely tempted to jettison his person, into the sea. The ship, driven off course, finally anchored in Antigua in the West Indies. There, Coke and his three companions, met with much kindness from the local Methodists, and were even invited to dine with Prince William Henry, later King William IV (1830-37). Coke preached on several islands—on one occasion to a thousand negroes, his first real experience of missionary work—and he considerably strengthened the Methodist cause there. On 10 February he sailed for Charleston. Upon reaching the American mainland his missionary labours were resumed with added gusto, and he rode 300 miles a week, preaching every day. After three months he returned to England to plead the cause of the West Indian mission to the British Conference: he also visited the Channel Islands with Wesley. During the course of the year he preached far and wide in England, and assisted Wesley with his administrative chores. He made collections for the missions, and he even went begging from door to door—the 'vile drudgery' as he called it. Countless hours were spent in this work, and thousands of pounds were collected. Even Wesley was led to remark that the 'doctor is too warm'.

In between visits to America and the West Indies, Dr Coke would occasionally return to the town of his birth, and he would use these occasions to visit the graves of his father and mother, and to preach in the town hall and in St Mary's church. A humorous story is related of how, when he was staying at a friend's house in the Watton,[2] and was preparing to preach in the town church attired in cassock and gown, Lion, the house dog, took exception to the unaccustomed garb, and attacked the good doctor's ample calves. Terrified by this unexpected onslaught, Coke sought refuge in the wood shed from which retreat, to his embarrassment, he was only to be rescued by a young lady living on the opposite side of the road who had happened to hear his desperate shouts for help.

The French Revolution (1789) seemed to Coke to open doors to Protestant missionary enterprise across the Channel, and he now travelled to Paris hoping to establish a mission there. However, when it was discreetly hinted to him that unless he took a hasty departure, hanging would be his lot, he returned to England to continue evangelising there. Following his return from his fifth visit to America and the West Indies—he had sailed for these destinations on 1 September 1792—he visited Holland hoping to induce the Dutch to permit a Methodist agency to operate among the negroes of St Eustatius. This initiative, also, was to end in failure. Equally unsuccessful was his attempt to form a missionary colony in the country beyond Sierra Leone.

In 1791 Coke who, earlier in life, had been in favour of the disestablishment of the Anglican church now, without authority from anyone, proposed a scheme to enable Methodists to remain within her embrace with himself and Asbury as bishops. The scheme was submitted to the bishop of London, but, after considerable deliberation and consultation, he eventually refused to sanction it. Disappointed that this knock at the door of the established church had failed to produce re-admission for those Methodists who desired it, Coke turned his attention to Ireland where, on his initiative, preachers were sent in 1799 to preach in Irish.

Following another visit to the West Indies (this was his eighth crossing of the Atlantic) and greatly encouraged by the success of his Irish mission, Coke, in 1800, inaugurated missionary work in Welsh in the Principality. His frequent journeys through north Wales, when travelling to and from Ireland, had convinced him of the need to send Welsh-speaking Methodist preachers to that part of Wales and though, unknown to him, some pioneering work had already been undertaken in certain parts of Denbigh-

shire and Flintshire, it was his promotion of the idea which led the
Conference to send Owen Davies (1752-1830) and John Hughes
(1776-1843) to Rhuthun in August 1800.

Together with being John Wesley's chief lieutenant, superintendent of the Methodist Episcopal Church of America, and the
'father' of Methodist missions, Dr Coke was also involved with
literary pursuits. He was to produce a valuable commentary on
the Bible, a labour of love which took nine years to accomplish,
and which made considerable demands on his own pocket.
Furthermore, Sunday Schools occupied his attention, and he was
the first to establish such schools in Cornwall.

Considering the frenetic nature of his activities, particularly
the time spent in America and the West Indies—he once seriously
contemplated living in America—it is hardly surprising that it
was not until late in life that he got married for the first time. The
lady in question was Penelope Goulding Smith, the only daughter
and heiress of a retired solicitor in Bradford, Wiltshire. His new
situation in life did not in any way inhibit his work; in 1805 he
inaugurated a Home Mission for England, assisted in the
appointment of a missionary to Gibraltar, and introduced gospel
preaching among the thousands of prisoners-of-war then confined in English hulks. In 1808 his appeal for preachers to work
among the negroes in Africa evoked a ready response, and it was
in this manner that the Methodist Agency in Africa was established. However, Coke's affairs of the heart were to be plagued
by misfortune and extreme sadness. Penelope Goulding Smith
died on 25 January 1811; he then married, as his second wife,
Anne Loxdale of Liverpool. Tragically, after a year of wedded
bliss, she also died.

His final grand design was the evangelisation of India, an
ambition which he had entertained for some thirty years. This
was an objective that had always been opposed by the British East
India Company which, by the eighteenth century, had established
major trading posts at Calcutta, Madras and Bombay. Though
the primary purpose of the company was trade, it was ultimately
to be instrumental in bringing large tracts of land into British
hands, thus laying the foundations of British power and hege-

Birthplace of Thomas Coke

Courtesy of A. T. Thomas

mony in that great sub-continent. When Coke discovered that the British government intended creating a bishopric in India, he applied for the see, and indicated that he would be prepared to return to the bosom of the established church were he appointed. Again, the olive branch was rejected. Coke now urged the Methodist Conference, despite considerable opposition, to establish a mission in Ceylon, offering his own services and £1,000 to defray expenses. This generosity was enough to induce the Conference to approve the mission. Coke now delivered his farewell and, as it turned out, his final sermon at Portsea. The text which he chose was, 'Ethiopia shall soon stretch out her hands unto God'. At Brecon he had preached on the same theme.

The expenses that he incurred in his missionary work were very considerable, and were paid for, very largely, from the rents which he received from two properties in Breconshire: an estate at Coity, and the 'Shoulder of Mutton' inn, situated near his own birthplace in the High Street ot Brecon, and noted for its assoc-iations with the Kemble family.[3] Frequently it was the case that these rents were in arrears, and Coke was to be at his most ruthless when demanding immediate payment so that he could proceed on one of his missionary journeys.

Coke set sail in the *Cabalva* on his final voyage on 29 December 1813. The ship formed part of a fleet escorted by British men-of-war as Britain was still involved in hostilities with Napoleonic France. On 2 May 1814, feeling unwell, he retired to his cabin having remarked to a fellow missionary that 'he would be better tomorrow'. He died the following morning, and lies buried in an unmarked spot on the seabed beneath the waves of the Indian Ocean.

Thus passed away a man of indefatigable energy and deep dev-otion; a tireless pioneering worker for the Methodist mission. At times, his path through life was far from easy, and on many occasions he had looked death in the face. He had crossed the Atlantic, in both directions, on no fewer than eighteen occasions: he had been shipwrecked, and he had been taken prisoner by a French privateer. In America he had ridden thousands of miles through the untamed wilderness, pursuing an ever expanding frontier, and enduring with fortitude great hardships and priv-ations. But even on these journeys, Brecon was never far from his thoughts, and when, in preparation for his visit to India, he made his will, his wish was that he should be buried alongside his two wives in the Priory church of his native town.

Irrepressibly eager and enterprising, Coke was also tactless, ambitious and impetuous with the result that he met with many disappointments in life and incurred many animosities. However, these rebuffs did not sour him, or daunt his great spirit. His fail-

The Dr Coke Memorial Schools. The site is now occupied by Leos

ings were many, but his achievements far outweighed them all. Brecon can be truly proud of this son of hers for he left an indelible impression in the sand here, and in other worlds.

Over the years he has received a bad press, and even his biographers have failed to serve him well. But at Brecon, to honour his name, the Dr Coke Memorial schools were erected. The Rev. Edwin Thornley conceived of the idea, and on 19 October 1867 John Robinson Kay laid the foundation stone. These schools, opened in January 1868, cost £1,400, and so successful were they that in 1881 an additional schoolroom for the infant department was built. Another, and more enduring monument to him, is the Wesleyan Missionary Society. The Memorial Schools were to be reduced to ash by fire in 1890, but the Society still exists, and expends time, energy and money every year in providing for the spiritual needs of those seeking salvation.

NOTES

[1] There were altogether thirteen colonies stretching from Maine in the north to Georgia in the south, bounded on the east by the Atlantic Ocean and on the west by the Alleghany mountains.

[2] This house was to be occupied later by alderman H.C. Rich, justice of the peace.

[3] Infra, pp. 100-101

SARAH SIDDONS (1755-1831)

In Georgian Brecon there were abundant opportunities for relaxation, and time to indulge in pleasurable pursuits. In an attempt to alleviate the monotony of life, the urban gentry indulged in such pursuits and pastimes as society balls, horse-racing, hunting, bowls, fives, tennis and theatre visits. The theatre was a great attraction, and strolling players from the English border entertained the 'genteel' element within the town population. Indeed, without such patronage by the gentry the provincial theatre would not have been able to survive at all. The law was most unhelpful, as by the Licensing Act of 1737 players were liable to be punished as rogues and vagabonds, and ways had to be devised to circumvent this legislation, otherwise actors would not have been able to play at marts, fairs, horse-races and cock-matches, or entertain audiences with 'good plays and waggon loads of scenes and adopted habits'. Actors could elude the law's embrace by becoming 'lecturers'. Having put together a few observations on human nature, they could move from town to town playing in the great rooms at the rear of inns, in barns or gentlemen's houses.

Some of the English border companies which visited Wales in the second half of the eighteenth century were very respectable. One such company was established by John Ward, who took the London theatre as his yardstick in an attempt to win the support of polite society. His company came to Brecon in 1755, and played for eight weeks in May and June. The visit was to prove a momentous one because, during the company's stay, the 'incomparable' Sarah Siddons was born in 'The Shoulder of Mutton' inn. The building is now known as 'The Sarah Siddons'. However, it bears little resemblance to the inn where Sarah first saw the light of day, for the upper floor no longer juts over the street and an extension to the rear of the premises conceals what was once a massive exterior wall.

John Ward was no stranger to Brecon. He had visited the town on previous occasions since Brecon was part of the circuit. The visit to Brecon in 1755 was timed to coincide with the May fair when country people from far and wide would throng the narrow streets of the medieval town. A stay of two months was most unusual, for the company could be expected to take advantage of the improved weather conditions—in winter, the roads would have been virtually impassable—to move from town to town on the circuit. The prolonged stay would seem to be indicative of the high esteem in which the actor-manager was held.

An actor and hairdresser in Ward's troupe was Roger Kemble, who had joined the company in Birmingham in 1752. In 1753, at Cirencester, he had married Sarah, the manager's daughter. He was a suave, genial man and a Catholic; she a dignified and determined girl and a Protestant. According to the terms of an agree-

Sarah Siddons as Mrs Haller in *The Stranger*

From the portrait by Sir Thomas Lawrence

ment drawn up between them, the boys were to be raised in the father's faith, and the girls in their mother's. The match had been a runaway one, for Sarah Ward was a renowned beauty who could have married an earl but chose instead a 'poor player'. When the company's wagon, heavily laden with stage properties and the personal belongings of the Kemble family, rolled into Brecon in 1755, Sarah was big with child, and the protracted stay at the town was a great relief and comfort to her. The little room in the 'Shoulder of Mutton' was luxury compared with the discomforts of travelling in a jolting wagon over appalling roads.

The Brecon run ended on 3 July and the company then moved to Llandrindod for a week's performance at the New Spa, which was now attracting an increasing number of visitors. Roger Kemble, despite his wife's condition, travelled with the company, but Sarah stayed on at Brecon where, on 5 July, she gave birth to the town's most illustrious daughter, Sarah Siddons. She was not christened until 14 July, when the event was recorded in the parish register of St Mary's church, located only some fifty yards away. The entry in the register reads: 'Sarah, d. of George (*sic*) Kemble, a commedian, and Sarah, his wife'. Sarah was to be the eldest of eleven children born to Roger Kemble and Sarah Ward, and the birthplaces of their celebrated children provide some indication of the nature and extent of the circuit. Two were born in Brecon. Apart from Sarah, the first child, there was also Charles, the eleventh, born in the town in 1775. Sarah was to be followed in rapid succession by John Philip who was born at Prescott (1750), Stephen at Kington (1758), Frances at Hereford (1759), Elizabeth at Dorrington (1761) and Julia Anne at Worcester (1764). Four children, Mary, Catherine, Lucy and Henry, were to die young. In an era when medical science was still in its infancy, deaths in babyhood were not uncommon, and these were family tragedies which caused a great deal of heartache.

No sooner was the mother fit to travel than the infant child started on the first of those journeys which she was to continue to make for some sixty years or so, playing on both sides of the Welsh border. Sarah Siddons was to move along the roads and lanes of Brecknockshire, Radnorshire, Herefordshire, Worcestershire, Shropshire and Staffordshire, and at a tender age she would have learnt to endure with patience the hardships of the road. As the eldest child she would, furthermore, have been expected to help in the raising of her brothers and sisters as, one by one, they made their appearance; and she would also have shared in the family sorrow as tragedy struck again and again. It was a very hard and unsettled way of life, and the reception accorded to the company could vary from place to place. As a stage player herself, Sarah knew how it felt to be hooted at and derided by audiences which believed that actors were the emissaries of Satan. But she also had to come to terms with adulation, when the appearance of Kemble was hailed with genuine pleasure and delight.

Despite this nomadic existence, the education of his numerous brood was not entirely neglected by Kemble. Though the children were enrolled as members of the company, Sarah and the others did attend day schools in the towns and villages which the company visited. Certainly, there was a lack of continuity in the education provided, though the situation would have improved somewhat during the winter months when conditions severely restricted movement along the roads. Then the company would have played in the one place for a much longer period of time, and the children's education would thereby have benefited. At Worcester, in 1767, Sarah spent the winter at Thornloe House, where a Mrs Harries ran a boarding school for young ladies. For a girl of Sarah's sensitivity and reserve, experiences of school could be most unpleasant. At Thornloe, a pupil by the name of Clara Bentinct wrote to inform her mother that a new pupil by the name of Sarah Kemble had joined their number and was 'felt to be something of an interloper'. Having established the occupation of Sarah's parents, Clara continues: 'You can imagine my embarrassment, my dear Mama, at having extorted so damaging a confession, I thought it best to make a curtsey and return to the other young ladies who were awaiting my report'. However, it is heartening to discover that Sarah was to win their esteem through the help which she was able to provide with the school theatricals, the very accomplishment which, initially, had incurred their disapproval. Her mother also helped with Sarah's education, since she taught her daughter to play the harpsichord, and to sing sufficiently well to entertain audiences in the intervals between the acts of a play.

These early appearances on the stage provided Sarah with a useful apprenticeship. At the Theatre Royal, Brecon, her youthful appearance provoked uproar as the audience assumed that she was being exploited by the company. Confused, Sarah was about to make a hasty withdrawal when her mother appeared, led her to the front of the stage, and made her repeat the fable of the 'Boys and the Frogs'. The protesters were completely silenced, and she concluded to rapturous applause. She could also be usefully employed in the wings, and at Kington she was seen beating a pair of snuffers against a candlestick to simulate the clack, clack of a mill.

However, it was not until February 1767 that her name appeared on a playbill advertising a part in a play. This was 'Charles the First', and Miss Kemble played the part of the young Princess Elizabeth. The same playbill included the name of the man she was destined to marry. This was William Siddons, a Walsall man who had played in the Chester theatre in May 1772 and had joined Kemble's company shortly afterwards at Birmingham. Though Sarah's beauty had led to offers of marriage from many wealthy suitors, she had refused them all. Like her mother she preferred a 'poor player'. William Siddons, with his pleasing appearance and ingratiating manner, had won her heart but the parents, forgetting their own experience, were rigorously opposed to the match, and Mrs Kemble, the 'old lioness', kept a watchful eye on the young couple.

In 1772, at Brecon, matters came to a head. A new admirer had appeared on the scene, a wealthy squire, Evans of Pennant. It was rumoured that he had become infatuated with Sarah after hearing her sing 'Sweet Robin'. As a wealthy landowner his advances towards Sarah were welcomed by her parents, and Siddons was infuriated. He now proceeded to make a thorough nuisance of himself, and was dismissed from the company though he was allowed a benefit. During this performance he

Birthplace of Sarah Siddons

By courtesy of Gwyn Evans

appealed directly to a Brecon audience in a song of his own composition, entitled, appropriately enough, 'The Discarded Lover'. He declared that though Sarah had accepted him with the approval of her parents, they had abruptly changed their minds when it appeared that a Brecon squire was about to solicit her hand in marriage. His lament won him sympathetic applause from the audience, and it was with their plaudits still ringing in the air, that he retired backstage to his room, only to be greeted by an outraged mother who promptly proceeded to cuff his ears. Some of the offending stanzas ran as follows:

Ye ladies of Brecon whose hearts ever feel
For wrongs like to this I'm about to reveal;
Excuse the first product, nor pass unregarded,
The complaints of poor Colin, a lover discarded.

Not easily turned, she her project pursued,
Each part of the shepherd was instantly viewed;
And the charms of three hundred a year, some say more,
Made her find out a thousand she ne'er saw more.

Dear ladies avoid one indelible stain,
Excuse me, I beg, if my verse is too plain;
But a jilt is the devil, as has long been confessed,
Which a heart like poor Colin's must ever detest.

As it turned out Squire Evans was to be the discarded lover and he was to die an insolvent bachelor.

Following this episode the concerned parents decided that, despite the financial loss it would entail the small company, Sarah should be protected from the temptations which were inherent in the stroller's way of life during the more impressionable years of her adolescence. She now became a lady's maid to a Mary Greathead of Guy's Cliff, Warwickshire, who had formed a favourable impression of her at one of her performances in Warwick. Though her wages were low, the duties were not heavy, and she learnt much about genteel living from service with an aristocratic lady. Removed, also, from the arduous life of the stage, if only temporarily, Sarah was able to develop a robustness of body which was to serve her well in future years.

But absence only made the heart grow fonder, and Sarah's love for Siddons was not in any way diminished by thus being separated from him. Her emotions at this time were portrayed in a short poem of her own composition which demonstrated also that she had no little skill as a versifier:

> Trust me Strephon with thy love;
> I swear by Cupid's bow above
> Nought shall make me e'er betray
> Thy passion till my dying day.
> If I live, or if I die,
> Upon my constancy rely.

When Sarah penned these lines, little did she know of the trials, tribulations and sorrows that awaited her in the years ahead. Sufficient unto the day, however, her constancy was finally to be rewarded, for her parents ultimately relented and on 26 November 1773, at Holy Trinity church, Coventry, Sal finally wed her William. They now rejoined the company on circuit, and after her two years of refined living at Guy's Cliff, Sarah must have found it hard to adjust. Nevertheless, her passion for the stage enabled her to prevail over the hardships, and life, once again, became a procession of towns.

The young couple now joined another travelling troupe, well known at Cheltenham, called Crump and Chamberlain, and it was with this group that Sarah was to achieve considerable fame. It was after a performance of Otway's 'Venice Preserved' at Cheltenham that Sarah met a Miss Boyle with whom she formed a lasting friendship. The patronage of Miss Boyle was to be of value to Sarah in another sense, since Boyle's stepfather, Lord Bruce, was to send glowing reports to London of the young actress who was charming provincial audiences, and Garrick, who was the manager of Drury Lane, became mildly interested. In the summer of 1775 he dispatched his talent scout, Tom King, to Cheltenham, from where he sent an enthusiastic report to his master after seeing Sarah perform in Rose's 'Fair Penitent'.

Nothing, however, came of it and, disappointed, Sarah and her little family—a son, Henry, had been born in October 1774—continued on their rounds.

In August 1775 the Rev. Henry Bates, pugilist, duellist and critic was dispatched by Garrick to Worcester to assess Sarah's acting qualities, and in his letters he provides graphic descriptions of the roads he had to traverse in order to get there. In the theatre he managed to find a place near the wings and on stage, only three yards away, he saw the 'theatrical heroine', and watched with wonderment her performance of Rosalind. So enchanted was the clerical editor of the *Morning Post* that he sent a glowing report to Garrick: 'Her face is one of the most strikingly beautiful for stage effect I have ever beheld, but face and figure are nothing to her action and stage deportment, which are remarkably pleasing'. He warned Garrick that if he did not engage Sarah for Drury Lane immediately, she was sure to fall into the clutches of the 'Covent Garden Mohawks'. Bates advised Sarah to provide Garrick with a list of her leading characters, and she sent twenty-three, though there was no mention of her Juliet and Cordelia, so little did she appreciate the nature of her tragic genius at that time.

Sarah was, however, again with child, and in no condition to appear on the London stage. She was also in dire financial straits, and Garrick sent her £20 to help her over childbirth. An agreement was now signed engaging Sarah and her husband to appear at Drury Lane for a joint salary of £5 a week. On 5 November 1775 Sally was born, and a few weeks later Sarah made her way to London and Drury Lane, the Mecca of all actors.

On 29 December 1775, though her name was not printed on the playbill, Sarah made her first appearance as Portia in the 'Merchant of Venice' on the stage at Drury Lane. This first night was to prove a disaster as, overcome by nervousness, and not completely recovered from childbirth, she lost command of her voice and forgot her lines. This experience was to be repeated time and again as Sarah tried part after part, Julia in the 'Black-amor Washed White' and Mrs Strickland in 'The Suspicious Husband'. But such was the confidence that Garrick still had in her acting ability that he allowed her to play opposite him in *Richard III*. Sarah was completely overshadowed by the great actor, and the *London Magazine* reported that Mrs Siddons was a lamentable Lady Anne. Condemned by critics and audiences alike, Sarah, at the age of twenty-one, her pride deeply dented, turned once again to the provinces. What Sarah and Garrick had both failed to appreciate was that she was tragedy personified. She lacked the playful touch needed in comedy, and the plays in which she appeared were invariably such. A percipient London critic was to put his finger on the nub of the matter when he wrote: 'Having no comedy in her nature, she rendered that ridiculous which the authors evidently intended to be pleasant'.

The fact that she had played for a season at Drury Lane and acted opposite Garrick had provided Sarah with a certain cachet, and provincial managers were certainly ready with their offers. However, she still clung to the hope that she might be allowed to continue at Drury Lane but Sheridan, the new manager, could see no justification for renewing her contract. Later, Sarah was to confide to a friend: 'It was a cruel and stunning blow, overwhelming all my ambitions, and involving peril even to the subsistence of my helpless babes. It was very near destroying me'. The bitter disappointment of being dropped from the company played havoc with her health and for months she was very near to complete collapse.

However, her determination and innate toughness enabled Sarah to triumph over adversity, and when she returned to the strolling life she was determined to rebuild her reputation. Fate smiled on her once again in 1778, when John Palmer, the manager of the Theatre Royal in Bath, engaged Sarah for the winter season at a weekly wage of £3. At first she played supporting roles, but Palmer, recognising her genius, soon gave Sarah principal parts. Audiences responded warmly to her, and slowly her confidence and self-respect were restored. Sarah was to play at Bath for four seasons, and her circumstances there were infinitely more comfortable than anything she had experienced whilst on tour.

Bath possessed the finest theatre outside London, and during the four years she played there Sarah was to reign supreme on its boards. Amongst her most ardent admirers was the beautiful duchess of Devonshire, who spread Sarah's fame wherever she went. Sarah's greatest triumph at Bath was as Isabella in 'The Fatal Marriage'. Critics began to take notice again, and the *Bath Chronicle* described her as 'the most capable actress who has performed here for many years', and the general opinion was 'that such a voice, such judgment and such acting should never have been discarded by London Audiences'.

The days of hardship for Sarah would soon be over, for she was rapidly reaching the situation where life would become more than just a struggle for her daily bread. Accepted with warmth and enthusiasm by her audiences, she also came to be accepted socially by the exclusive Bath set, and prominent among these socialites was Mrs Piozzi, a close friend of Samuel Johnson. In 1779 Sarah gave birth to another daughter, Maria, and the demands of her ever-increasing brood meant that Sarah had to manage her finances very carefully; an attitude which later led to her being accused of being parsimonious. The upbringing of the children further meant that Sarah had to learn her parts in the small hours of the morning. For Brecon's famous daughter, life was still far from easy.

It was in 1780 that Sarah again met Thomas Lawrence, a handsome young man whom she had first met in Devizes years earlier. He had come to Bath to paint two portraits of the actress, and it was now that he met for the first time Sarah's two daughters, Sally who was six and the baby, Maria. Sarah little realised then that this feckless and irresponsible man was to bring great tragedy into her life. He was to befriend both girls, and become their escort to fashionable events in Bath. But this friendship was to develop into a deeper emotion; and he was to fall in love first with Sally and then with Maria, and when Maria became seriously ill, he transferred his affections back to Sally. William Siddons could provide little guidance or support, for he was in poor health—he suffered from gout—and in constant need of the waters at Bath. Sarah was experiencing one of the worst phases of her life, and her cup of unhappiness overflowed in October 1798 when Maria died. Sarah's husband now began to speculate foolishly, and he squandered £10,000 of her hard-earned savings. In an attempt to recoup this loss, Sarah embarked on what turned out to be a most profitable tour of Ireland, leaving the ailing Sally in the care of her father at Bath. By the time Sarah returned from the tour (March 1803), Sally was dead. Sarah and her William had come to the crossroads. An indifferent actor himself, he had always envied his wife's success, and he had increasingly come to resent being known as 'Mrs Siddons' husband'. What is remarkable is that Sarah remained constant to this petulant, cantankerous, bitter, and rather worthless man for so long. He died in 1808 with Sarah at his bedside.

In 1782 came the long awaited summons. On 10 October, at twice her former wage, Sarah made her second appearance at Drury Lane, now under Sheridan's management. The play chosen was Thomas Southerne's tragedy, 'The Fatal Marriage'. The day was spent in a torment of anguish; she was torn by alternating feelings of fear and hope. Everything was at stake—her reputation, her future, together with that of the family. Sarah was to describe how, in the dressing room allocated to her, 'in one of what I call my desperate tranquillities, which usually oppress me under terrific circumstances, I there completed my dress, to the astonishment of my attendants, without uttering one word, though often sighing most profoundly'. When she walked on stage to face 'that immense space, lined as it was with human intellect from top to bottom', the old nervousness returned. Gradually the tenseness disappeared, and she forgot herself and her audience; she became Isabella, and as the drama unfolded, the anguish which she was able to communicate to the audience led to its being seized by an intense excitement. One who was present describes the degree of enthusiasm as surpassing anything which he had ever experienced. Women swooned and had to be carried away; strong men were heard to sob loudly and unashamedly, and the whole house shook to the applause. Sarah had returned; Sarah had conquered; the capital lay at her feet. The following day the press trumpeted her praises, and ladies of fashion besieged the theatre to buy tickets for the pit. From that moment Sarah Siddons was to shine forth as the tragic muse of England.

For the next thirty years Sarah was to dominate the English stage to an extent that no other actress before or since has been able to achieve. Audiences were electrified by her performances, and she had absolute control over their emotions; they cried when she cried, and smiled when she smiled. On stage the impression that she created was extraordinary. She was fêted and lionised by high and low alike, and illustrious painters, like Sir Joshua Reynolds and Gainsborough, were to capture her on canvas and poets to sing her praises in verse. The adoration she received was enough to turn the head of any actress, but through it all Sarah remained singularly unaffected. Proud, haughty and regal she might appear in public, yet in her private life Sarah remained simple and unspoilt. There was nothing she liked better than a quiet night at home with her family and friends. But Sarah's success and popularity excited envy, and malicious tongues were at work; for the remainder of her life she had to endure this vicious gossip. It must have been deeply humiliating to her to read in a newspaper that, 'Consols, Stocks, Siddons, Teas have all fallen these last two months, and are likely to fall still lower in the public esteem'. Such was the price of fame; the pedestal to which she had been elevated was to prove a most uneasy resting place.

Until she was thirty Sarah had never played Shakespeare. Her triumphs had been in popular plays like 'The Fatal Marriage', 'The Grecian Daughter', 'The Fatal Interview', 'The Fair Penitent', and 'Venice Preserved'. This situation was grist to the mill of unsympathetic critics, who were not slow to hint that she was purposely avoiding the immortal bard. Sarah was to prove them all wrong. She was to give incomparable performances of Shakespeare's heroines, though it was as Lady Macbeth that she attained the peak of her acting powers. Leigh Hunt described the sleepwalking scene as one of 'bewildered melancholy', and one of the most sublime pieces of acting ever seen on the English stage. On one occasion in Scotland it was received so rapturously that Sarah had to perform it all over again. It was as Lady Macbeth that Sarah was to appear at her farewell benefit night on 29 June 1812.

After the sleep-walking scene the audience insisted on the curtain coming down. Sarah was to perform in public on only two occasions after that memorable night of triumph: in 1817, when her powers were waning, as Lady Macbeth for her brother Charles's benefit, and in 1819 as Lady Randolph in 'Douglas', again for the same purpose.

Despite her successes in England, on her first visit to Scotland, during her season in Edinburgh, Sarah failed to melt Scottish hearts. However, on her second, she broke through the barriers, and won the same rapturous reception north of the border that she was accustomed to receive in the south. It is recorded that the church synod arranged its meetings so as not to conflict with any of her performances, and on one occasion 2,550 people applied for the 650 seats available.

In her late forties, aware that her beauty could soon wither on the vine, Sarah enjoyed one brief romantic interlude with a handsome fencing master by the name of Galindo. It may have been nothing more than an indiscreet friendship, but when the liaison became generally known, it did considerable damage to the reputation of the stage goddess held in such veneration. Sarah was to complain bitterly of the 'malicious vipers' damaging her good name, and it was only after a hard struggle that she was able to restore her tarnished image.

But the years were catching up with Sarah, and when she was in her fifties, though her acting was still mesmerising audiences, and she could still command a fee of up to £50 for a single performance—a great deal of money in those days—her obesity was beginning to make her look ludicrous in some of the costumes which she had to wear. At one performance her stoutness was to prevent her from rising from a chair in which she had wedged herself. By 1811 it was becoming increasingly difficult for Sarah to play through a long scene, and the critics were beginning to comment adversely. Crabb-Robinson wrote that 'her advancing age is a real pain to me and her voice appears to have lost its brilliancy'. Her great beauty fading, her voice weakening and her dramatic powers waning, Sarah was conscious that her days of glory were over. But she was to draw on all her reserves for that magical retirement performance in 1812 when, literally, she brought the house down. If only she had left on that high note, because critics were unamimous in their belief that the occasional appearance which she made on stage after that night was mistaken.

In her charming *Records of My Girlhood*, Sarah's niece, Fanny Kemble (Mrs Butcher) recalled that breathtaking performance in 1812. She recounts how her father had taken her in the early morning to witness the dense crowd outside Covent Garden Theatre waiting for the doors to open. She recollects being in the theatre at the commencement of the performance when a solemn female figure in black appeared 'and the tremendous roar of public greeting that welcomed it'. The Georgian theatre was small and there was, consequently, a certain intimacy between players and audience. Gestures, facial expressions and voice inflexions were indispensable adjuncts of the actor's art, and these were skills which Mrs Siddons possessed in abundance. It should also be remembered that Sarah was weaving her magic upon critical audiences without the assistance of elaborate stage properties, period costumes, and sound effects which are now the stock-in-trade of the theatre. She was usually carelessly attired; often her costume was incongruous as in the 'Grecian Daughter' when she appeared in hoops, high-heeled boots and powdered hair.

In her retirement Sarah was a lonely, dispirited woman. After her successes, the accolades, the paeans of praise from all quarters, she was now an empty shell; a queen without a throne. In her mind's eye she lived and relived the scenes of her triumphs. Interest in her, however, gradually diminished, and she found it difficult to adapt to her new role. In May 1831 Fanny Kemble, after a visit to her aunt, wrote: 'Drove to my Aunt Siddons. Every time I see that magnificent ruin some fresh decay makes itself apparent in it, and one cannot but feel that it must soon totter to its fall. What a price she has paid for her great celebrity—weariness, vacuity, and utter deadness of spirit'. Even if one accepts that this was the rather jaundiced view of a young observer, the impression still remains that Sarah was in decline.

But Sarah Siddons was not entirely lost in a sea of loneliness, weariness and despondency. She developed a new outlook on life, and became reconciled to the idea of old age and its limitations. This new philosophy was enshrined in the following lines of verse:

Say, what's the brightest wreath of fame,
But canker'd buds, that opening close;
Ah! What the world's most pleasing dream,
But broken fragments of repose?

Lead me where Peace with steady hand
The mingled cup of life shall hold,
Where Time shall smoothly pour his sand
And Wisdom turn that sand to gold.

Together with her daughter, Cecilia, and her faithful maid, Patty Wilkinson, Sarah lived for a while at Westbourne, a country residence in Middlesex. But in 1817 she moved to 27, Upper Baker Street, a substantial house in London overlooking Regent's Park. In an attempt to alleviate a generally mundane life style, she gave parties and readings in its spacious rooms, but she still found the evenings that she spent alone long and weary.

It was at her London home, after a week of acute suffering that, on 8 June 1831, Sarah Siddons died from erysipelas. On 15 June she was buried in the graveyard of Paddington church, and over 5,000 people from all stations in life, attended the funeral. The simple inscription on her tombstone read:

Sacred to the memory of Sarah Siddons, who departed this life June 8th, 1831, in her 76th year. Blessed are the dead which die in the Lord.

On the north side of the chancel of Paddington church there is also a plain mural tablet bearing the same words, and in Westminster Abbey, the final resting place of the great and the good, is to be found her memorial statue, approached 'thro' rows of warriors and thro' ranks of Kings'. Sarah Siddons fully deserves her place amongst the celebrated of the land.

THEOPHILUS JONES (1759-1812)

This marble but records his name—the history of this, his loved, his native County, will long survive and be his monument.

Theophilus Jones was born in the ancient marcher town of Brecon on 18 October 1759, and on the 8 November following he was baptised in St Mary's church. He was the only son of Hugh Jones, curate of St David's church, Llanfaes, who resided in a charming house in Lion Street where George Bull, the saintly bishop of St David's, had died earlier in the century.[1] In 1763 Hugh Jones became vicar of Llangamarch (1763-8) and, subsequently, in 1768, of Llywel (1768-99). In addition to these livings he held a prebend at Christ College. His wife, Elinor (died 1786) was the eldest daughter of Theophilus Evans, vicar of Llangamarch between 1738-63, a living which he resigned in 1763 in favour of his son-in-law. Evans was a literary figure of great distinction, and his *Drych y Prif Oesoedd,*[2] a rather prejudiced and uncritical, yet most entertaining, account of the early history of Wales, is regarded as one of the great classics of Welsh prose. On 8 June 1739 he was inducted vicar of St David's in Brecon, a living which he held until his decease in 1767.

Much of Theophilus Jones's boyhood was spent at his grandfather's house at Llwyn Einion, Llangamarch, and there can be little doubt that his antiquarian tastes were first awakened, and then fostered, by him. From his grandfather, to whom he was very attached, he inherited, also, many historical documents which were to be of considerable value to him later when he was compiling his famous *History*.

While his maternal grandfather was certainly a great formative influence in his life, his more formal education was undertaken at Christ College, Brecon. Here, the headmaster at the time, was the Rev. David Griffith. He had been appointed to the post in 1757, and he helped to promote a much needed renaissance in the school's fortunes during a century when the College, for the most part, was stagnating. David Griffith was an accomplished scholar of whom, in later years, Theophilus was to write warmly that he was 'the respected and respectable preceptor of my youth'. Christ College was populated very largely by gentlemen's sons, and Theophilus was to establish close ties of friendship with many of them, a factor which was to be of inestimable benefit to him when writing his monumental work. A luminary at the College, who became a lifelong friend, was Edward Davies (1756-1831), later to be nicknamed 'Celtic Davies'. Following a period 1783-1799 as master in Chipping Sodbury grammar school, Gloucester, he became curate of Olveston in the same county. He is now best remembered as the author of two works dealing with Celtic subjects—*Celtic Researches* (1804) and *The Mythology and Rites of the British Druids* (1809). It was these works that were to give birth to his byname. Though fate was to decree that they should follow divergent paths, Theophilus was to correspond regularly with his school friend, and this relationship was only finally to be severed by death. Under Griffith, as headmaster, Theophilus would have received a thorough grounding in the classics—Latin and Greek—and these skills would, undoubtedly, have been a valuable asset to him as a historian and antiquary.

It was his parents who decided that he should embrace the study of the law, and to launch him on this career he was articled to Penoyre Watkins, a solicitor with a very large practice in Brecon. The choice of Penoyre Watkins was not the product of chance; he had married a not too distant cousin, one of the Lloyds of Rhosferig. On completion of his articles, Theophilus Jones branched out on his own, and became a successful and highly respected solicitor and attorney in his native town. Though there is reason to believe that he had little natural inclination for his profession, he practised as a solicitor for a considerable time, and when a vacancy occurred in the deputy-registrarship of the archdeaconry of Brecon, he was appointed to the post. A wealth of historical material of incalculable value now came his way, for amongst the papers committed to his care were the records of the various parishes in the archdeaconry, and as his chief delight was in literary studies and antiquarian research, these were indeed grist for the mill.

Theophilus took as his wife Mary, the daughter of Rice Price of Porth-y-Rhyd, near Llandovery, in Carmarthenshire. Her mother, also a Mary, was the daughter of Daniel Williams of Llwynwormwood. On their marriage Theophilus and his wife lived in a large and comfortable house in Mount Street, now known as 'The George'. The rooms were oak-panelled and lofty, and there they resided until the decease of Theophilus's father when they removed to his house in Lion Street where the *History* was written. This, also, was a spacious habitat, and in a letter which he wrote to the Rev. Edward Davies on 4 October 1801, he exclaimed in great excitement: 'I've such a room! such a study! . . . it is at the back part of the house, no noise or interruption, except now and then a call into the office . . . I laugh, I laugh at the imps of gloominess'. The Rev. Hugh Jones had died on 2 April 1799 and was buried with his wife Elinor, who had preceded him earlier on 24 July 1786, in St David's churchyard. The death of his father which, despite the sense of grievous loss, left him materially better off,[3] may well have helped to determine the course of action that he now embarked upon, and that was to write a history of his beloved county of Brecknock. However, he soon discovered that it was impossible to combine a busy career as a solicitor with writing the *History*. And so, with the full approval of his wife, and the assurance of a small income of his own, he now relinquished his practice and, living upon his private means, devoted himself entirely to his writing. This decision was to result in his losing upwards of £400. The practice was easily disposed of to his partner, Samuel Church of Ffrwdgrech, but as his researches would involve him in the examination of old wills and deeds, he reserved the office of deputy-registrar in his own hands. It was not until 1809 that he finally found himself in a position to declare, doubtless with considerable satisfaction: 'Done with the law'.

Unhampered by the restraints of employment, Theophilus Jones now threw himself heart and soul into his researches, and he spared neither time, nor expense nor himself in the accom-

Theophilus Jones's house in Lion Street
Courtesy of Brecknock Museum

plishment of what had become his life's ambition. He personally visited every parish in the county, laboriously copying down inscriptions from church monuments and walls many of which, with the passage of time, and as a result of restoration work, have since disappeared for ever. From the older inhabitants he gleaned information about folk-lore and ancient legends; repositories far and wide were targeted and visited, and Hugh Thomas's 'Essay towards a History of Brecknock' was thoroughly plundered. His contacts with the leading gentry families within the county enabled him to trace their genealogies with a reasonable degree of accuracy, and these family trees formed an integral part of the *History*. His effort was untiring, his patience inexhaustible, and his delving thorough and painstaking.

However, despite the wide range of his contacts, and his friend-ships with notable people, the birth of *The History of Brecknock-shire* was still to be accomplished only with considerable difficulty. For all his love of history and antiquities, Theophilus was very conscious of his own deficiencies for the task, especially his lack of formal training. He once described the work 'as foreign to my profession, though congenial to my feelings and my pursuits.' His search for information, and his inquiries, resulted in his being viewed with grave suspicion in many quarters. He remarked: 'Should the Historian seek access to them (documents) and should that Historian unfortunately be of the profession of the law, . . . suspicion is alive and prudence bolts the door against the intruder, who it is supposed can have no other motive for his inquiries than the discovery of objections to titles, the propagation of scandal, or the abrasion of old sores which have long cicatrized'.

Despite the impediments Theophilus still found among the nobility and gentry many who were most supportive, and he paid particular tribute to the Duke of Beaufort and Sir Charles Morgan of Tredegar Park for their generous contributions towards the expenses incurred in producing the work. A more general thanks was extended to those 'respectable noblemen whose time was so completely occupied in the service of the State, or the duties of the Senate, that it became inconvenient to them to return a written answer to my application, I am indebted for their good wishes, as well as their benevolent intentions of contributing a few eleemosynary guineas towards the expense of the publication and the support of the publisher, which have been occasionally most kindly communicated to me by their agents; and to many of the gentlemen and inhabitants of the county who were really anxious that I should prosecute what they considered as a public utility, and who were ready to assist in the execution of it, I return my most unfeigned thanks'.

The first volume, published in 1805 by Messrs William and George North of Brecon, was dedicated to the Rev. Thomas Payne, rector of Llanbedr and Partricio and vicar of Defynnog 'as an acknowledgement of the assistance he has received and in testimony of the friendship which he feels as proud thus publicly to avow as he is happy in private life to experience'. The cost to subscribers of this part of the *History* was £2 12*s*. 6*d*. and it has been estimated that between 400 and 450 copies were produced. The second volume, issued in two parts, was dedicated to another close associate, Edward Davies: 'To the Rev. Edward Davies of

Olveston, in the County of Gloucester, author of *Celtic Researches* etc, the associate of his youth, the kind correspondent and assistant in his literary pursuits, the sincere friend in mature age, and oh! may he add, in trembling hope, *si modo digni erimus,*[4] the partaker of a blessed eternity, this volume is gratefully inscribed by the author'. The second volume was priced at £4 to subscribers so that possession of both volumes meant a total outlay of £6 12*s.* 6*d.*, a considerable amount of money especially in those days. It is quite apparent that these were volumes designed for the shelves of libraries in gentlemen's houses and not for the humble abodes of the labouring classes. The preface to the second volume was devoted to rebutting criticisms of the first, though Theophilus did find space to thank several gentlemen for their assistance.

A second edition of his *History* in one volume, though with some additions, was published by Edwin Davies in 1898 and at a price which brought it within reach of a larger circle of readers. In 1909-11 Davies began bringing out a third edition which was completed in 1930 by the County Historical Society. To enable Theophilus's *History* to be brought more up to date, these four volumes contained information taken from the collections of the first Baron Glanusk, who had been Lord Lieutenant of Brecknockshire. The Glanusk edition is an indispensable source book for all students of Brecon and Brecknockshire.

Theophilus's general narrative closed with Henry VIII, though the parochial section was carried forward to about 1800. His volumes represented the first attempt at a county history in the Principality, and were also the first sizeable books to be printed and published in the county. Since then other county histories have made their appearance, but his is still regarded as the best. In the first edition there were many typographical errors as the author had had no experience of proof reading. This situation was compounded by errors relating to historical facts and dates. Edward Williams (Iolo Morganwg) condemned vitriolically the innumerable errors allegedly made by Theophilus Jones. Thomas Price, however, had immediately leapt to his defence declaring that, 'Mr Jones, whilst preparing his work for the press, was so grievously afflicted with gout that his left hand had to support the wrist of his flannel-bound right as he guided the pen, with the tips only of his fingers at liberty, while severe twinges of pain every now and then arrested his progress, and under such circumstances it is wonderful that the mistakes were not still more numerous'. Furthermore, his prejudices, as demonstrated by the scant attention which he pays to notabilities like John Penry and Dr Coke, were only too apparent—his anti-popery, his dislike of Dissent and Methodism, and his prosaic nature which meant that he was blind to the merits of Henry Vaughan as a poet.

However, his antiquarian interests were not confined to the *History*. He was also the author of an unpublished English translation of that outstanding Welsh literary prose jewel, *Gweledig-aethau y Bardd Cwsg*.[5] Moreover, he had contributed several papers to the short-lived *Cambrian Register*, edited by Dr William Owen Pughe, and to *Archaeologia*, and his intention had been to write a history of neighbouring Radnorshire, a design which he was only prevented from accomplishing by his ill health. Further, in his possssion was a manuscript copy of Aneurin's 'Gododdin', a gift from Anthony Bacon. Following his decease the book passed into the hands of another close friend—despite the great disparity in age—Thomas Price. Price (Carnhuanawc),[6] when his family was resident in Builth Wells had, in 1805, entered Christ College, Brecon, as a student. He had lodged in the town, and was a regular visitor at Theophilus Jones's house in Lion Street at the time when Theophilus was engaged in writing the second volume of his *History*. Many of the drawings for the illustrations in this volume were largely his work. The intimacy between Theophilus and the young man had arisen from the fact that Price was the son of Theophilus's old friend, the Rev. Rice Price, vicar of Llanwrthwl.

But Theophilus, despite his deep involvement with his *History*, still found time to participate actively in local affairs. He was a committed freemason, and was mainly instrumental in the formation of the Cambrian Lodge in 1789 at the 'Swan Inn', Ship Street. Invested Worshipful Master then, he was to occupy the chair until 1804. Attendance at these early lodge meetings was appalling, though there would not appear to have been a shortage of suitable candidates. During his fifteen years in the chair, Theophilus was to hold fifty meetings of the lodge, and of these thirteen had to be adjourned owing to 'insufficient Brethren being present'.

His zeal for education was demonstrated by the fact that he was a subscriber to the Brecon Benevolent Schools which began their work in 1811, and he was also chapter clerk at Christ College, whose welfare he always endeavoured to promote. When, in 1809, a single trust was established for the county known as the Breconshire Turnpike Trust, included in the ranks of the Trustees, all prominent men in the life of the county, was Theophilus Jones.

Theophilus Jones: a drawing by Thomas Price

After a long period of intense suffering, Theophilus Jones died on 15 January 1812 at his house in Lion Street. His decease at such a young age—he was only fifty-two—is attributed to repeated attacks of gout, the scourge of the leisured classes in those days. Such was his affliction that in his later years he could walk only with the greatest difficulty. He was buried at Llangamarch, and was interred in the same grave as his grandfather, Theophilus Evans, whom he had always revered. In Christ College, Brecon, where he had spent many a happy hour as a pupil, his widow erected a white and grey marble tablet in his memory.

Following his death, as his wife had not borne him any children,[7] his library, which contained a large and valuable collection of books, was disposed of by public auction 'on the premises at Brecon' by a Mr Wise of Bath. The sale occupied three days and many of the volumes—there were 1,220 altogether—had been annotated by Theophilus. Some of the volumes were to fetch very good prices. The copyright of his *History*, together with the copper plates and some manuscript collections, was purchased by George North, his publisher, for £255.

His passing was deeply lamented, for Theophilus Jones was a generous friend and greatly esteemed by those who knew him. As a lawyer he had been upright in his dealings with his clients, and he was never prepared to sacrifice his convictions on the altar of advantage. He was kind, affable and good-humoured; hospitable but never ostentatious in his style of living; and, towards the less fortunate members of local society, extremely benevolent. A devout Anglican, he had embraced the tenets of the church from a deep sense of conviction though, unfortunately, it left him myopic when he came to consider those whose religious views differed from his own. His love of Wales—and he was Welsh-speaking—was deep, but his affection for his own *bro* was boundless and passionate. Theophilus Evans, his mentor as well as a much loved relative, would have been well-pleased with his grandson.

NOTES

[1] George Bull had been appointed bishop of St David's in 1705 by Queen Anne when he was seventy years old. Because of his knowledge of the early fathers, he was regarded as 'one of the glories of anglican scholarship'.

[2] A mirror of the First Ages (1716).

[3] In 1789 his annual income amounted to £434, a not inconsiderable sum.

[4] If only we shall be worthy.

[5] Visions of the Sleeping Bard.

[6] Thomas Price (1787-1848) was born at Pencaerelin in Llanfihangel Bryn Pabuan, Brecknockshire, the younger son of Rice Price, vicar of Llanwrthwl. He was ordained a priest on 12 September 1812, and in April 1813 he moved to Crickhowell to take charge of the parishes of Llangenny, Llanbedr Ystradyw and Partricio. To these were added in 1816 the neighbouring parishes of Llangattock and Llanelli. In 1825 he received the vicarage of Llanfihangel Cwmdu, augmented in 1839 by the curacy of Tretower. He continued to live in Crickhowell until 1841 when he built a house for himself in Cwmdu. He was undoubtedly the foremost Celtic scholar of his day. In addition to his literary pursuits, he was also a highly skilled craftsman, especially in metals.

[7] He did, however, have an illegitimate son, David, born about 1781 who became a naval surgeon. He lived at Plymstock in Devon and died in 1864.

ADELINA PATTI (1843-1919)

'A nightingale once sang a song that rang across the world'.
Ethel Rosate-Lunn[1]

In the upper reaches of the Swansea valley, above Abercrave, on an eminence overlooking the river Tawe, is to be found the imposing mock castle of Craig-y-nos. A house was built there between 1841-3 by Rhys Davies Powell, a retired Indian Army Officer, and a member of the wealthy Glyn-llech family which claimed descent from Gwladys, one of Brychan Brycheiniog's numerous daughters. Rhys Powell, in 1835, had married an heiress, Sarah Dolmage King, and the new house which he built for the family was designed by T.H. Wyatt of London, the architect also responsible, about the same time, for the shire hall, Brecon. Following the death of Brychan Powell, Rhys's eldest son, the estate passed into the hands of his two sisters, Jane and Gwladys, and they, in turn, sold it in 1875 to a Mr Morgan Morgan, a prominent local landowner and industrialist, for £8,000. In 1878, Morgan sold the estate to Adelina Patti, and she was to spend an estimated £100,000 in enlarging the original house, purchasing more land, and landscaping the grounds. This greatly extended and much beautified house, for more than thirty years, was to become 'Home Sweet Home' to one of the greatest sopranos that the world has ever known.

It is quite possible that Patti's attention was drawn to the possibilities of the house at Craig-y-nos by Sir Hussey Vivian, M.P. (later Lord Swansea), and his brother Graham Vivian, when she stayed with them at their home, Cadoxton Lodge, Neath. The house appeared to meet her two basic requirements: first, to satisfy her lover Nicolini's desire to live the life of a country gentleman, for he had a particular fondness for fishing and shooting; and secondly, to provide herself with a stately, elegant and secluded retreat. That Swansea tradesmen were involved in the refurbishing becomes apparent from a letter written by Patti in Paris to a Mr Blanchard of Swansea on 16

Adelina Patti

Courtesy of Brecknock Museum

April 1880 in which he is instructed to 'please to have laid down carpets in all the master bedrooms, these carpets must not cover the whole of the floor: it must be left uncovered all round the room in a width of one metre, or in English measure one yard and a quarter: these carpets are to be of very good quality but not too dear'. Not only was her chateau to be furnished exactly as she wanted it; there was also to be strict budgetary control. It further becomes evident from the letter that two years after the purchase the house was still not ready for occupation.

The new owner of the property at Craig-y-nos, Adelina Patti, was not indigenous to the area, for she had been born in Madrid in Spain in 1843. Her mother, a denizen of Rome, was the fiery Caterina Barili, a soprano with four children by a previous marriage, whilst her father, a hot-blooded Sicilian, was Salvatore Patti, a tenor, and their main claim to fame was that, together, they had brought Patti into this world. Patti was very proud of her Italian parentage, and whenever asked what nationality she was—and this was a question put to her repeatedly—the reply left little room for doubt: 'Italian! Italian! true I was born in Madrid but because a man is born in a stable that doesn't make him a horse'. Legend has it that there was drama even at her birth, for it is averred that her mother started in labour towards the end of a performance of *Norma* at the Royal Opera House, Madrid. She was taken to the greenroom where she gave birth. The date was 10 February.[2] In actual fact Caterina never played *Norma* during that Madrid season. Adelina was born at 6, Fuencarral Street, the house of a general's wife, and it was at 4 p.m. on Sunday, 19 February 1843, that the world heard her very first trill. Some six weeks later she was christened Adela Juana Maria but she was to be better known as Adelina Patti.

Patti made her first acquaintance with America when she was only four. The family had emigrated to the States and taken up residence in New York. There the mother sang regularly in the new opera house, while the father became involved with operatic management. The young Patti was taken to the opera house whenever her mother sang, and these experiences were to exercise a profound influence on her. After being tucked up in bed with her dolls, she would get up and give her own make-believe performances. So vivid was her imagination that, to simulate an audience's possible reaction, she would even throw herself nosegays which she had made from old newspapers. Even at this stage in her development the future diva was not lacking in confidence.

Adelina's genius was to blossom early. It soon became apparent to the parents that the child possessed a remarkable musical talent and that they had a prodigy on their hands. Their eyes were opened to her exceptional gifts when, at the age of seven, using the kitchen table as a stage, she gave a rendering of 'Casta Diva' from Bellini's *Norma* which amazed her parents. But Adelina was to be launched on to the public stage earlier than could normally be expected because of a financial crisis in the Patti family. Her father's foray into management had proved a disaster, and to feed his numerous brood he had been compelled to pawn some of the family valuables. Appreciating the great talent possessed by their daughter, the parents saw in Adelina a means of extricating themselves from their very real troubles. And so Adelina's career was launched, and she was to have the satisfaction and joy of seeing the pawned items restored, one by one, to the family home.

Adelina's public career began in 1850 and ended in 1906, the longest reign of any artiste. Between 1850-57 she performed as a juvenile and undertook two tours: the first between 1850-3, when she travelled across America and visited Canada, Mexico and Cuba. Her obsession with dolls was demonstrated at Cincinatti when she refused to appear on stage until she had been provided with one. Throughout the tour she was to remain faithful to them, and was quite indifferent to the large sums of money—her share of the takings amounted to $20,000—she was earning. The second tour took place in 1857 when she visited the southern states of America and the West Indies. However, her operatic début was made at the age of sixteen when she performed in the title role of 'Lucia di Lammermoor' at the New York Academy of Music. Her performance took the house by storm, and the *New York Herald* praised her 'high soprano voice, fresh and full and even throughout'.

In 1861, accompanied by her father and brother-in-law, Maurice Strakosch, Adelina arrived in England and gave her first operatic performance there at Covent Garden, when she sang 'Amina' in Bellini's *La Sonnambula*. Since she was a comparative unknown, the house was far from full, and her appearance was greeted with what may be described as a sympathetic round of applause. However, her London début proved to be the most brilliantly successful by any artiste in the nineteenth century. It raised the audience to a high pitch of excitement, and she concluded to a hurricane of applause and recalls. The long reign of possibly the world's greatest prima donna had begun, and London lay at the feet of the Queen of Song. The 'Patti Craze' manifested itself, and police had to be summoned to control the crowds that thronged around the stage door. The season was to enhance Adelina's reputation and, by royal command, she sang before Queen Victoria at Buckingham Palace; an invitation which was to set the seal on Adelina's fame. Charles Dickens, the eminent novelist, was one who heard Adelina sing, and he joined the list of those paying homage before her throne. His impression was that she possessed 'not only great and welcome promise but also that talent for success—charm'.

The London season was followed by a short European tour, which included performances at Berlin, where she captivated King Wilhelm, who became one of her greatest admirers, Brussels and the Hague. In Holland Adelina demanded a fee of 3,000 francs for a single performance, an amount which had to be authorised by the Dutch cabinet before payment could be made. Adelina did not come cheap.

Following the 1862 season spent at Covent Garden when every performance was a sell-out, Adelina returned to Europe and sang at Paris and Vienna. Napoleon III and his Empress were so delighted with her performance in Paris that they invited her to the Imperial *loge*, where they presented her with a magnificent bracelet studded with diamonds and emeralds. In Austria the Emperor Franz Joseph attended her every appearance at the Karl Theatre, Vienna, and he even presented himself backstage to address his compliments. Even more acceptable to Adelina, however, was the jewellery that he showered on her. Everywhere she was received with adulation, and there were occasions when she was in danger of being crushed by the admiring crowds. For the twenty-year-old the reception was overwhelming, and in an interview with *Figaro*, the French newspaper, she was to confide: 'if you only knew how fond I am of quiet'.

Adelina's pattern of life now involved performances at the London opera followed by a continental tour. She took a house in Clapham, a suburb of London, then fairly rural in aspect, and for five years, between engagements, she stayed at this villa. She was still being guided by her father and Strakosch for her mother, after Adelina's American triumphs, had returned to Rome and did not share in her daughter's success. In 1865 Karolyn Baumeister, 'Karo', was engaged by Adelina and she became her constant companion for the next thirty-five years.

On 5 July 1865 Adelina gave a concert at the newly erected St James's Hall, Regent Street. Her repertoire included 'Home Sweet Home' and 'Comin' thro' the Rye', which became her theme songs. It was towards the end of this year that she paid her first visit to Italy, her parents' native land, and her countrymen flocked into the theatres at Florence, Bologna, Rome and Turin, where they were reported to have 'shouted and applauded and wept like children with sheer delight'.

1866 was to prove a fateful year in one respect at least. In May, at Covent Garden, when he played 'Edgardo' to her 'Lucia', Adelina had made the acquaintance of a handsome French tenor with the stage name of Ernesto Nicolini. His real name was Ernest Nicolas, and he was a thirty-two year old native of St Malmo. He was a married man and father of five children. His voice having disappointed—Adelina had not been favourably impressed either, and neither was she impressed by his vanity and womanizing—his contract was cancelled, and he returned to Paris. However, he was to reappear in London in the spring of 1871, when he came over to England with the flood of refugees fleeing the siege of Paris by German troops. Nicolini's voice being, by now, much improved he was engaged as a permanent member of the company at Covent Garden. The Frenchman had re-entered Adelina's life.

When Adelina was in Paris she was frequently a guest at Court, and attached to the imperial entourage was a dapper little man by the name of Henri, Marquis de Caux. His official status was equerry to Napoleon III. He was the head of a noble, but by no means wealthy, family, his annual income being £400. Adelina may possibly have had lovers already; she had certainly received many offers of marriage, but these had been treated with indifference. However, when the marquis started paying court, she was swept off her feet by his eloquent tongue and refinement of manner. Furthermore, the liaison was fostered by their mutual interest in music and dancing, the marquis being renowned for his gracefulness on the dance floor. The couple were betrothed in the spring of 1868, and married in the Roman Catholic Church, Clapham Common, on 29 July. Adelina now lived in Paris, and despite the disparity in age—he was her senior by eighteen years —the first two years of marriage passed tolerably well. Thereafter, the relationship began to deteriorate, and they began to quarrel incessantly. Possibly her emotional involvement with the marquis had never been deep, and there were those who believed that the diva had loved the coronet more than the man. By 1877 the marriage, to all intents and purposes, was over, and they were formally separated. By the terms of the final settlement in the divorce proceedings made on 15 July 1885 the marquis was awarded 1,500,000 francs. Adelina was free, but she had paid a high price for it both socially and financially. As for the marquis, he did not live long to enjoy his windfall for, on 13 December 1889, he died. The winter of 1868 had witnessed Adelina bewitching audiences in St Petersburg and Moscow, and the Tsar Alexander had come under her spell to such a degree that he appointed her 'Imperial Court Singer' and awarded her the the Order of Merit.

Adelina and Nicolini were now appearing on stage together. In June 1876 she played 'Aida' to his 'Ramades' in the London premiere of Verdi's work. Both performances were quite exceptional and, gradually, Adelina's feelings towards Nicolini changed from a cold indifference to love. During their tour of Italy in 1878, when they appeared in Milan, Genoa, Florence, Rome and Naples, Adelina's affair with Nicolini was brutally exposed when his wife, with the help of some assistants, finally caught up with him, and the newspapers regaled their readers with lurid descriptions of Nicolini, to his great discomfiture, being booted down a flight of stairs. However, the tour itself was a success and people, to see her in the flesh on stage, slept in the streets and public squares. Verdi was to describe her performances in these words: 'She is an artist by nature, so perfect that perhaps there has never been her equal'.

The sensational disclosures of their adulterous affair, which resulted in her being ostracised by high society for transgressing strict moral codes, may well have been another reason for the lovers seeking 'an oasis in the desert'. Certainly it was at this time that, in collaboration with Nicolini, Adelina purchased Craig-y-nos. He was now to become her husband as well as her lover, for no sooner had Adelina gained her divorce than she quickly married him. On 9 June 1886 there was a civil ceremony before the French Consul in Swansea, and on their return to the castle at Craig-y-nos, they received addresses of congratulations from various local bodies. The following day, a religious ceremony, conducted by the rector, the Rev. E.L. Davies-Glanley, was performed at the Anglican Church in Ystradgynlais before a full congregation, and in the bright glare of publicity. The pair were to live very happily at their 'chateau', and Adelina's lifestyle can best be described as regal, befitting the Queen of Song.

Adelina's triumph in Italy, despite the scandal of her liaison with Nicolini, was followed in 1881 by a return to the country of her infancy. It was optimistically held that her box-office success in Europe would be a harbinger to similar success across the Atlantic. The tour proved a fiasco, and the problems arose from an uncharacteristic lack of trumpet-blowing and poor planning. It was only after Adelina had agreed to sing for a charity, and the price of seats had been halved, that there was a revival of business.

1882 saw Adelina in America again. She had been persuaded to return by the impresario, Colonel Mapleson, who argued that it was not her voice that had been responsible for the failure in 1881 but the lack of organisation. On this occasion nothing was left to chance, and the diva sang to full houses. Her remuneration was handsome indeed, for she was paid £900 for every performance, and it delighted opera buffs to calculate the amount she earned for every note she sang. Her growing attraction to opera lovers can be gauged from the fact that when singing in Vienna in 1863 her fee had been £1,000 a month.

Like Thomas Coke, Adelina was now crossing and recrossing the Atlantic regularly. She was yet again in America in 1883, a visit which coincided with the great rivalry for operatic supremacy between Mapleson's Academy of Music and the newly opened Metropolitan Opera managed by Henry Abbey. Adelina was the ace in Mapleson's hand. She delighted audiences and critics alike, and on 16 November 1883 it was reported in the *Daily Graphic* that: 'one might as well attempt to criticise and analyze the warbling of the nightingale as to discover defects in her voice'. Mapleson recorded one humorous incident associated with Adelina at Boston. The guaranteed fee for the performance was $5,000 but Mapleson had only managed to collect $4,000 and when Franchi, Adelina's agent, reported this to the prima donna she agreed to present herself at the theatre, but she would not appear on stage. Mapleson frantically collected a further $800, and Adelina then agreed to put one shoe on but still insisted on remaining in her dressing room. It was only after the impresario had found another $200 that Adelina slipped on the other shoe and walked smiling on stage.

Though Adelina was the trump in Mapleson's hand, an intense rivalry had developed between her and another gifted soprano at the Academy, Etelka Gerster. Gerster became her *bête noire* and, according to Adelina, she was possessed of an evil eye. Gerster's malevolent powers were such that if any mishap occurred in Adelina's presence, she would immediately attribute it to her rival, and shriek her name. On one occasion, while walking along a darkened corridor before Gerster's hotel bedroom, and wishing to neutralize the effects of any evil vibrations emanating from within, Adelina extended the first and fourth fingers of one hand, and in the process nearly struck Gerster's husband in the forehead as he bent to place his shoes outside the door.

In America Adelina travelled by train in considerable comfort. Her railway carriage was sumptuous. Built at a cost of $60,000, it had heavy silk damask curtains at the windows, gilded tapestries on the wall, and bathroom taps of solid silver. It even boasted a Steinway piano. A travelling companion of Adelina was a pet parrot, a gift from Nicolini, who had trained the bird to swear in French and to squawk, 'Cash! Cash!' whenever Mapleson appeared. In California, 'Opera madness' and 'Patti fever' manifested themselves, and people resorted to all kinds of stratagems in order to hear her sing; they even removed slates from the roof of the opera house and literally dropped in. It has been estimated that from her American tours of 1883 and 1884 Adelina earned around $500,000.

During Adelina's tour of America in 1884 there was intense rivalry of a different kind. While Italian opera was presented at the Academy, the Metropolitan had embraced German. On 26 November Adelina performed in *Marta* at the Academy in what was booked as the twenty-fifth anniversary of her operatic début.

Ernesto Nicolini
Courtesy of Brecknock Museum

The event was heralded with the usual American razzmatazz. A dinner was arranged in Adelina's honour by some musical critics and prominent New Yorkers, but the occasion was soured by the absence of the wives, who declared that they could not be seen associating with a 'fallen' woman. The 1884-5 tour was to have been Adelina's last visit to the States, and she herself had informed a reporter of the *New York Daily Tribune* that she felt 'that America should have only my best and that the Country where I first was received with open arms when a mite of a child should not remember me as a worn-out singer'. The visit did not turn out to be anything of the kind, and Adelina was to visit America again on no fewer than six occasions.

In the summer of 1886 Adelina was engaged to sing in four concerts at the Royal Albert Hall. They proved a resounding success and huge profits were realised. The 'Patti Concerts' had been launched, and for decades they were to attract thousands of people to the colossal hall at Kensington Gore. At these concerts she would sing the evergreen 'Home Sweet Home', which always evoked a profound emotional response with the audience leaning forward and hanging on to every note.

Nicolini now decided that there was an untapped vein in South America, and he made arrangements for Adelina to perform there. In December 1887 she travelled via Paris and Madrid to Buenos Aires. Her fee was £1,000 a performance and a percentage of the profits. She gave twenty-four performances, and it has been estimated that she received, altogether, £38,400, making her the highest paid artiste at that time. In 1889 Adelina returned to South America, and her fee had now risen to £1,250 a night, together with a percentage of the profits. In Mexico Adelina was welcomed with the kind of adulation which one now associates with a superstar, and women pawned their trinkets and jewellery in order to buy tickets. President Diaz even presented her with a solid gold crown.

Adelina, however, had not forgotten her Welsh 'chateau', and when the opportunity presented itself, between her lengthy and demanding tours, she would appear at Craig-y-nos to 'recharge her batteries'. Adelina was at her castle in 1889 when the National

Eisteddfod was held at Brecon, on Cerrig Cochion Hill, the big pavilion being erected on the site subsequently occupied by the Girls' Grammar School. Adelina visited the Eisteddfod on the afternoon of the second day. She arrived by train from Penwyllt,[3] and the band of the South Wales Borderers was dispatched to the Brecon station to greet her. The route between the station and the pavilion was lined with thousands of people who cheered wildly as she drove past. When the party accompanying the great diva entered the pavilion, the entire audience rose as one person to a deafening roar of welcome. As Adelina herself ascended the platform, leaning on the arm of Dr James Williams, coroner of Brecon, another great cheer went up. Adelina, having been presented with a bouquet of flowers by Lord Tredegar, then turned to face the audience and bowed her acknowledgement of the plaudits. It was only after she had taken her seat that silence was restored. The vast audience, estimated at some 12,000 people, was then addressed by Dr Williams who wished the most famous of nightingales a long and untroubled life:

> Hir, hir einioes,
> Yn hollol ddi-loes,
> I'r enwocaf eos—
> Patti Craig-y-nos.[4]

The prima donna now enraptured everyone with some Italian arias, and as a first encore she sang, 'The Last Rose of Summer', and to the request for a second she sang another great favourite of hers, 'Home Sweet Home'. But then it was that Adelina cast a spell over all present, and won the heart and soul of an entire nation. She sang the Welsh National Anthem, 'Hen Wlad fy Nhadau', while the audience, led by Mabon,[5] the miners' leader, contributed a chorus. At its conclusion Adelina was accorded a reception the like of which for its spontaneity and genuineness could scarcely have been equalled anywhere.

In 1891 the small theatre which Adelina had had built in the new wing[6] at Craig-y-nos was opened before an invited audience of friends and dignitaries, and it was to prove the jewel in the crown. It was a replica of the famous opera house at Bayreuth,

Germany, and was planned and designed by two Swansea archit-
ects. To the accompaniment of a little orchestra imported from
Swansea, Adelina and Nicolini sang from *Traviata* and *Faust*
much to the delight of all present. She was to use the theatre not
only to entertain her friends, but also to develop her skills at
miming. Sir Augustus Harris, impresario of the Royal Opera,
Covent Garden, and the manager of Drury Lane, told Adelina
that if she had not been the world's greatest singer, she could
easily have been one of its best actresses. The theatre, which could
seat about 150 people, was erected by a Swansea builder and
consisted of a ground floor, orchestra pit and dressing rooms.
The pit could be raised to the same height as the floor, and the
floor itself could also be raised by mechanical means from its
slight gradient until it was entirely level. The auditorium could
then be converted into a handsome ballroom. All the seats were
upholstered in blue velvet, and the walls were decorated in
honour of the great composers whose works she had performed.
At Christmas time there was always a tree there heavily laden with
gifts for the staff graded in order of importance. In the evening
there would be a staff dance—Adelina loved the waltz—and she
would take the floor with the chef, butler and footman, while her
consort would dance with the head girls.

Adelina was in America again in 1891-2, 1892-3, and 1893-4.
The latter tour was a dismal failure. She was suffering from a per-
sistent cold, the country was in recession, and her supporting
artistes were mediocre. Some critics wrote of her performances
with pens dipped in vitriol. Adelina, understandably, cut short
her tour and returned home where in December 1894, much to her
delight, she gave a private concert to Queen Victoria at Windsor.
She spent the night at the castle and before Adelina left, a grateful
Queen presented her with a fine brooch-pin engraved with the
royal crown and monogram.

Following the disappointment of her last tour of America,
Adelina turned her gaze once again towards Europe, and in 1895
she sang in Germany and the south of France. She was now fifty-
two, and while celebrating her birthday she was able to contem-
plate with satisfaction that she had been in harness for forty-five

years; she was really beginning to believe what people were saying about her that 'she was a wonderful little woman'.

In June 1895 Adelina made the first of six appearances at Covent Garden which were described as triumphs. Indeed, the first was described as a 'triumph without flaw'. Her appearances on the operatic stage now came to an end—her last public appearance as an operatic singer occurred in the winter of 1900 at Covent Garden—henceforth she was to follow a routine of concert performances in London, the provinces and the south of France. At this time Nicolini's health was beginning to fail; he was troubled by disorders of the liver and kidneys. He availed himself of various 'cures', but to no good effect. So ill did he become that when Adelina was made an honorary burgess of Brecon on 24 May 1897, he was unable to accompany her to the ceremony. He

Casket presented to Adelina containing the freedom of Brecon

died at Pau in France on 18 January 1898 with Adelina at his bed-side. The scroll which conferred on her the freedom of the borough was contained in a casket carved from a piece of oak taken from the roof of the Priory church, and the honour was conferred on her in 'recognition and acknowledgement of her eminent and her munificent services to the poor of Brecon'.

Adelina was not to wear her widow's weeds for long, for she was now to take a third husband when she was only a few days short of her fifty-sixth birthday. In the summer of 1897 a tall, slim and exceedingly handsome man had been her guest at Craig-y-nos. In November 1898 he was her companion when she appeared at the Royal Albert Hall. Her beau was Rudolph (Rolf) Ceder-strom, a thirty-seven year old Swedish baron, and the director of a health gymnasium in London. Whilst her first husband, Henri, had been her senior by eighteen years, Rolf was her junior by roughly the same number of years. In modern parlance he was her 'toy boy'. A short courtship was followed by marriage at St Michael's Roman Catholic Church, Brecon, on 25 January 1899, an event treated as a civic occasion by the town fathers. The union brought Adelina a title and her spouse a fortune. Adelina had been more successful at acquiring husbands than begetting children, and she was to die childless. Cederstrom, however, following Adelina's death remarried, and his new bride was to present him with a daughter.

While Nicolini was alive, the champagne had flowed like water at Craig-y-nos. Dances, elaborate dinner parties, and musical and theatrical entertainments had been the order of the day. Cederstrom's influence, however, was like a dead hand. These events became things of the past. It would appear that Ceder-strom disliked many of Adelina's friends and they were no longer made welcome at the castle. In 1901 she put her house on the market because she and her husband wished to spend more time with his family in Sweden. Adelina was also beginning to suffer from rheumatism, and her doctors had advised her that the con-dition was possibly linked to the damp atmosphere of the Swansea valley. No attractive offers were received, and the option was withdrawn. The couple travelled a great deal in

Europe, and performances were still given at the Royal Albert Hall. In 1903 she crossed the Atlantic yet again. This tour, while proving a financial success—her fees were pre-guaranteed—was an artistic failure, and in Philadelphia a concert had to be postponed because the ticket sales were not sufficient to make it a viable proposition. People even rioted when trying to reclaim their money. Adelina, understandably, was never to visit the States again.

In 1905, after much persuasion, Adelina agreed to have her voice recorded for posterity. Her reluctance arose from her aversion to this new fangled toy, which she felt would not do justice to her voice, an assumption which, unfortunately, was to be borne out by events. She received a fee of £1,000, and to create a studio at Craig-y-nos two adjoining bedrooms were used. The recordings sold at just over £1 each, a sum which represented the average weekly wage at that time. By modern standards—the technique after all was only in its infancy—the voice reproduction is of very poor quality, though Adelina, when she first heard herself on record, was quite captivated. However, it is undoubtedly true that her reputation as one of the world's greatest sopranos has been somewhat sullied by people's disappointment at the cruel distortions which now pass as Adelina's golden voice.

Adelina, during her closing years at her 'beloved' home at Craig-y-nos, pursued a relatively quiet life-style. She seldom sang, though she played a great deal on the piano, the castanets and the zither. There was a piano in almost every room; even the bedroom was provided with one. She disliked rain, and on such occasions she would maintain that she wished her chateau had been built on the Rhine. Seldom did Adelina appear before lunch but then, leaving the castle by the front door, she would walk round to the winter garden[7] stocked with tropical trees and plants. From there she would proceed to the aviary,[8] and thence to the conservatory and dining room which adjoined it. In the late afternoon, accompanied by her maid, Odile, she would take another stroll which sometimes took her down to the lake where she would sit watching the swans.

The chateau over which the chatelaine presided so graciously

Craig-y-nos Castle

Courtesy of Brecknock Museum

was large, commodious and set in several acres of beautiful grounds. In the years immediately preceding the outbreak of the first World War in 1914 there were eighteen regular staff within the castle itself—the house steward and his wife, Adelina's two personal maids, three housemaids, three laundry maids, a chef who was a *cordon bleu*, three kitchen maids, butler/valet, two footmen, and an odd-job man. They constituted a closely knit community, and a family atmosphere prevailed at Craig-y-nos.

Together with the household staff, there were also the ground-staff, and these included four gardeners in permanent residence and a few others who came in daily. Their services were needed because all kinds of fruits and vegetables were grown at the castle's large gardens. The winter garden, conservatory and hot houses had also to be cared for, and, in the hot houses, peaches and grapes were grown, together with orchids and gardenias. Furthermore, the castle boasted a magnificent rose garden and, at the bottom of the terrace, a fine rock garden. As with most

large houses in the Victorian age, there was the inevitable lake.
Actually, there were two at Craig-y-nos, the old and the new. The
old was the boating lake, and on it were to be found two boats, the
'Trout' and the 'Mary Anne'. In the spring the beautiful lawns
before the pavilion, near the tennis courts, were a wonderful
sight, being surrounded by thousands of daffodils, while in the
same season the lawns at the front of the castle were always
planted out with wallflowers edged with forget-me-nots.

One of the finest rooms in the castle was Adelina's drawing
room, or salon as she preferred to call it. Here were assembled the
treasures from her countless tours, including autographed photo-
graphs of the crowned heads of Europe; here she could relax and
relive her triumphs with the clamour and cheering of audiences
ringing in her ears.

The castle had its own private chapel provided with an altar, a
pew and stained glass windows. It was always decorated with
beautiful flowers, and Adelina permitted Odile and other Catholics on the staff to make use of it. Those of the staff who were
Protestant attended the church at Callwen. There, two pews were
reserved for the exclusive use of the castle staff, one for the men
and the other for the girls. Since the services were conducted
mainly in Welsh—only once or twice a month were they conducted in English—most of the girls employed at the castle, who
were English in speech, were not regular attenders.

Physically, Adelina was petite—she was five-foot-two-inches
tall with a seventeen-inch waist—and extremely beautiful. She
was a brunette with large, brilliantly expressive, dark eyes.
Sartorially, as befitted her regal status, she was elegantly and
expensively attired. She possessed beautiful evening gowns, the
very latest modes from Paris, the fashion centre of Europe. These
dresses provided the perfect setting for her magnificent jewellery,
many of the pieces gifts from wealthy admirers and suitors. Her
favourite colours were black, white, or a very pale shade of some
other hue. Adelina was very proud of her small, dainty feet,[9] and
her stockings were made of heavy silk, and matched exactly the
dress and shoes which she happened to be wearing. Her hands
and arms were covered by long gloves which she changed

frequently, and in her later years, in order to disguise the ravages of time, she was heavily made-up, and she also wore a wig.

As a personality Adelina, though always dignified, was possessed of a bright and lively temperament, and was brimful of sparkling humour. Despite her world-wide fame, she remained unassuming and unaffected. But she could be wilful and quick-tempered, and if someone or something incurred her displeasure, she would literally explode. However, the storm would soon abate, and calm would be restored. Despite the occasional tantrum, she was extremely kind and benevolent towards her staff, and they repaid her with their total devotion and loyalty. Though the wages she paid them were low—a maid who had just started working at the castle received £3 a month—there were other compensations. There was always an abundance of food and retiring staff were provided with pensions.

At Craig-y-nos the conventions of the age were strictly observed. Staff were not permitted to take any liberties, and Adelina was addressed as 'My Lady' and Cederstrom as 'My Lord'. The maids wore long black dresses and little white lace caps. My lord and lady always dressed for dinner, and a screen was drawn across the dining room so that they could not be observed eating.

Riches were greatly coveted by Adelina; and from her singing she was to amass an immense fortune, which was advantageously invested for her by her friend, Alfred de Rothschild. For her, status and wealth were inextricably bound together; they went hand in glove; she could not have the one without the other. Expensive clothes, jewellery, and a magnificent home, were the trappings of success. She was extremely proud of her God-given talents, and vanity was a trait not foreign to her nature. Her pride, arrogance even, was demonstrated when the directors of the Norwich Musical Festival expressed a wish to engage her. Concerned about the level of her fee, they asked why she charged so much for a Musical Festival. To this request Adelina simply replied: 'I am a Musical festival'. Her vanity, on the other hand, was manifested in an innocent manner at Craig-y-nos by her obvious delight and satisfaction when people passing the castle, stopped, obviously hoping to see the great prima donna in the flesh. Adelina certainly enjoyed her celebrity status.

Though Adelina was endowed with a great natural talent, nurtured by a musical home background, she still had to work hard to perfect her voice. It was only after having her voice trained over many years that she was able to attain that degree of perfection which made her the wonder of the world. Diet formed an integral part of the training, and she did not eat anything which she felt might impair the quality of her singing. To Adelina diet did not imply limiting the amount of food she consumed, for she ate heartily. Rather was she careful about what she ate. High on her list of priorities were white meat and vegetables, white wine and soda, and the occasional glass of champagne. Pepper she did not take at all.

The diva was an extremely intelligent woman, blessed with a remarkable memory and the gift of repartee. Amongst her many talents was her linguistic ability, for she spoke six languages— English, French, German, Italian, Spanish and Russian. There was nothing cold, impersonal or aloof about her. She loved associating with people, and she was particularly fond of little children. On her numerous walks in the vicinity of the chateau, there was nothing she liked better than to converse with the people that she met, irrespective of whether they were tramps— these were usually dispatched to the kitchen for some sustenance —workmen, or the 'genteel' element. She loved dogs, and her pets were provided with stone-built and slated kennels and led very pampered lives.[10]

During her years at Craig-y-nos, despite her numerous official engagements, Adelina endeared herself to the local populace through her generosity and philanthropic activities. Her kindness to children was exemplified by her practice, every Christmas, of providing refreshments for hundreds of those living near her home, and, in a letter dated 21 December 1892, she mentioned having entertained 3,000 for tea. The old and the needy were not forgotten either: 'Yesterday I gave my annual distribution of money to all the poor old people of the district—it was a most touching sight and everyone, myself included, cried'. Hospitals at Brecon, Neath and Swansea were further supported, and in 1882 she gave the first of her charity concerts at Swansea when £830 were raised. Following this event, concerts were given, with tolerable regularity, at all three towns and the profits, which averaged between £700 to £800, would be donated to such institutions as the Brecon Infirmary, the Swansea General Hospital, and the Rest and Convalescent Home at Porthcawl. The distressed at Brecon and Neath were also helped for at both towns she established Poor Funds for their support. On those occasions when Adelina sang to sustain her charities, the town hosting the event would be bedecked with flags and a holiday proclaimed. She would be met on arrival by the mayor and corporation and, following an address of welcome, would be conducted to the festive board; all to a background of wildly enthusiastic crowds. On one occasion, piqued at hearing that the prices of tickets for a charity concert which she was to give at Swansea—either at the Albert Hall or the Grand Theatre—had been lowered since her previous visit, she boycotted the town and sang instead at Cardiff. On 20 June 1912, in recognition of her efforts on behalf of the poor, Adelina was made a 'Freeman' of the borough of Swansea, the first woman to be so honoured. She was to make her last public appearance on 20 October 1914 at the age of seventy-two, when she emerged from retirement to sing at a concert held at the Royal Albert Hall in aid of the Red Cross War Fund at which King George V and Queen Mary were present. Adelina, like Sarah Siddons, both true thoroughbreds, finished in style.

In her old age Adelina suffered increasingly from rheumatism and heart problems, and her serenity had also been disturbed by the Great War (1914-18). On Saturday 27 September 1919, at the age of seventy-six, she died clasping her husband's hand. Her local physician, Dr Watson of Abercrave, was also at her bedside. The following day, the body was embalmed, and after lying at rest in the chapel at Craig-y-nos, and in the Roman Catholic Chapel at Kensal Green, London, she was buried at Père Lachaise Cemetery, Paris, on 29 May 1920. It was at her own request that she was interred at Père Lachaise for buried there also were her father and her sister, Amelia. Père Lachaise was a final resting place which Adelina was to share with Rossini and Chopin, composers for whom she had the greatest admiration.

[1] She was head laundry maid at Craig-y-nos between 1909-14.

[2] The story originated in the fertile imagination of the tenor, Jose Sinico with some assistance from Adelina's brother-in-law and early manager, Maurice Strakosch.

[3] She had built her own private road to the station where there was a waiting room for her exclusive use.

[4] A long long life, wholly untroubled, to the most famous of nightingales, Patti, Craig-y-nos.

[5] William Abraham, 1842-1922.

[6] Apart from the theatre, the new wing contained bedrooms, dressing rooms, a gun room and the chapel. Infra p. 142.

[7] This building was presented to the County Borough of Swansea by Adelina in 1918, just a year before she died, to commemorate the close ties between her and the town. It was dismantled in 1919, and brought to Swansea on a relay of twenty lorries. Re-erected in Victoria Park, it was opened to the public in 1922.

[8] Following Adelina's decease in 1919, the aviary was presented by Baron Cederstrom to the London Zoological Gardens.

[9] She wore size two shoes.

[10] I am indebted to Mrs 'Winnie' Thomas, who was a maid at Craig-y-nos during the last few years of Adelina's life, for much of the material relating to her routine at the castle.

BIBLIOGRAPHY

A *Background*

Bindoff, S.T., *The House of Commons 1509-1558*, London, 1982.
Davies, Rupert, E., *Methodism*, Harmondsworth, 1963.
The Dictionary of Welsh Biography, Down to 1940, London, 1959.
Jenkins, Geraint H., *The Foundations of Modern Wales 1642-1780*, Oxford, 1987.
Id., *Hanes Cymru yn y Cyfnod Modern Cynnar 1530-1760*, Cardiff, 1983.
Jenkins, R.T., *Hanes Cymru yn y Ddeunawfed Ganrif*, Cardiff, 1945.
Jones, Theophilus, *History of the County of Brecknock*, ed. J.R. Bailey, Brecon, 1909.
Poole, Edwin, *The Illustrated History and Biography of Brecknockshire from the Earliest Times to the Present Day*, Brecon, 1886.
Price, Cecil, *The English Theatre in Wales*, Cardiff, 1948.
Rees, Thomas, *History of Protestant Nonconformity*, London, 1883.
Richards, Thomas, *The Puritan Movement in Wales, 1639-53*, London, 1920.
Id., *Religious Developments in Wales, 1654-1662*, London, 1923.
Williams, A.H. *Welsh Wesleyan Methodism, 1800-58*, Bangor, 1935.
Williams, David, *A History of Modern Wales*, London, 1969.
Williams, Glanmor, *Recovery, Reorientation and Reformation: Wales, 1415-1642*, Oxford, 1987.

B *Specific*
Books

Brinn, David, *Adelina Patti*, Bridgend, 1988.
Butler, H.E., *The Autobiography of Giraldus Cambrensis*, London, 1937.
Campbell, Thomas, *Life of Mrs Siddons*, London, 1839.
Cone, J.F., *Adelina Patti: Queen of Hearts*, Aldershot, 1994.
Crowther, J., *The Life of the Rev. Thomas Coke, Ll.D.*, Leeds, 1815.
Etheridge, J.W., *The Life of the Rev. Thomas Coke, D.C.L.*, London, 1860.
Evans, W.O., *Thomas Coke, Y Cymro a'r cenhadwr*, Bangor, 1912.
Ffrench, Yvonne, *Mrs Siddons, Tragic Actress*, London, 1954.
Giraldus Cambrensis, *The Itinerary through Wales and the Description of Wales*, tr. Richard Colt Hoare, Everyman's Library, 1908.
Hughes, H.J., *The Life of Howell Harris*, Newport, 1892.
Jones, Thomas, *Gerallt Gymro: Gerald the Welshman*, Cardiff, 1947.
Klein, Herman, *The Reign of Patti*, London, 1920.
Morgan, E., *Life and Times of Howell Harris*, Holywell, 1852.
Nuttall, Geoffrey F., *Howel Harris 1714-1773: The Last Enthusiast*, Cardiff, 1965.
Pierce, William, *John Penry, His Life, Times and Writings*, London, 1923.
Roberts, G.T., *Howell Harris*, London, 1951.
Williams, David (Ed.), *John Penry: Three Treatises concerning Wales*, Cardiff, 1960.
Williams, Samuel, *John Penry 1563-1593*, Cardiff, 1956.

Essays and Articles

Carr, A.D., 'Welshmen and the Hundred Years War', *Welsh History Review*, IV, 1968.

Davies, Conway, 'Giraldus Cambrensis, 1146-1946', *Arch. Camb.*, XCIX, 1947.

Davies, Gareth, 'Trevecka', *Brycheiniog*, 15, 1971.

Davies, John, 'Howell Harris and the Tevecka Settlement', *Brycheiniog*, IX, 1963.

Davies, Samuel, 'Thomas Coke, Ll.D.', *Y Geninen*, 1886.

Downey, David S., 'Madame Patti and Craig-y-nos castle', *Brycheiniog*, 24, 1990-2.

Jones, T. Rhys, 'Theophilus Jones, F.S.A., 1759-1812', *Brycheiniog*, 5, 1959.

Ker, Neil R., 'Sir John Price', *The Library*, 5th series, X, No. 1, 1955.

Morgan, F.C., 'The Will of Sir John Price of Hereford, 1555', *N.L.W. Journal*, IX, No. 2, 1955.

Richter, M., 'Giraldus Cambrensis', *N.L.W. Journal*, XVI, 1969-70.

Roberts, Gomer M., 'Gleanings from the Trevecka Letters', *Brycheiniog*, 2, 1956.

Id., 'Gleanings from the Trevecka Letters', *Brycheiniog*, 3, 1957.

Rosate-Lunn, Ethel, 'My Recollections of Madame Patti', *Brycheiniog*, 7, 1961.

Vickers, John A., 'Thomas Coke of Brecon (1747-1814)', *Brycheiniog*, X, 1964.

Walker, David, 'Gerald of Wales', *Brycheiniog*, 18, 1978-9.

Id., 'Gerald of Wales, Archdeacon of Brecon', *Links with the Past, Swansea and Brecon Historical Essays*, Llandybie, 1974.

Williams, Glanmor, 'John Penry a'i Genedl', *Grym Tafodau Tân*, Llandysul, 1984.

Index

Abbey, Henry, 133
Abercrave, 125, 145
Abergavenny, 82
Abergwili, 88
Abraham, William (Mabon), 136
Acts of Parliament:
  Act of Supremacy (1534), 21, 31
  Acts of Union (1536-43), 28-9
  Act of Supremacy (1559), 34
  Act of Uniformity (1559), 34, 53
  Act for the Better Propagation and
  Preaching of the Gospel in Wales
  (1650), 58-9
  Riot Act (1715), 73
  Conventicle Act (1664), 73
  Licensing Act (1737), 99
Agincourt, battle of, 16
Alpha Chapel, 71
America, xv, 86, 90-2, 93, 94, 96, 127,
  128, 132-5, 137, 140
Anderson, Anthony, 48
Angharad, 1
Asbury, Francis, 90, 91-2, 93

Bacon, Anthony, 121
Baldwin (archbishop), 3, 5, 6, 8
Bancroft, Richard, 47
Barili, Caterina, 127, 130
Barlow, William, 36
Barnes, Joseph, 38, 41
Bates, Henry, 107
Bath, 108-9, 110
Battle, battle at, 1
Baumeister, Karolyn (Karo), 130
Benevolent schools, 122
Bevan, Arthur, 74
Bevan, Bridget, 74
Black Death, 13
Boleyn, Anne, 21
Brecknockshire Agricultural Society, 80
Brecon, xiv, xv, 1, 6, 8, 10, 13, 14, 15,
  23, 25, 31-2, 60, 61, 63, 73, 74, 76, 80,
  82, 83, 86, 87, 88-9, 92-3, 96, 98, 99, 101,
  103-5, 109, 115, 116, 121, 122, 123, 125,
  136, 138-9, 145
Bren, Llywelyn, 14
Bristol, 56, 76, 79, 90
Brychan, 6, 125
Builth Wells, 71, 121
Bull, George, 115 and n

Cabalva, 96
Caerphilly, 76
Callwen, 142
Cambridge (university), 22, 24, 37
Carquit, William, 3
Catherine of Aragon, 21
Caxton, William, 43
Cecil, William, 48, 49, 52, 53, 54
Cederstrom, Rudolph (Rolf), 139, 140n,
  143, 145
Cefn Brith, 35, 36
Charity schools, 66
Charles I, king, 56, 58
Charles II, king, 61
Christ College, 36, 88, 115, 116, 121, 122,
  123
Church, Samuel, 117
Circulating schools, 67, 69
Claggett, Nicholas, 68
Coke, Bartholomew, 86-8
Coke, Thomas, xiv, xv, 86-98, 121, 133
Court of High Commission, 40, 46
Covent Garden, 107, 113, 129, 130, 131,
  137, 138
Craig-y-nos, xv, 125, 127, 132, 135,
  136-7, 139, 140-2, 143, 144, 145
Crane, Mrs Nicholas, 43
Crecy, battle of, 13
Cromwell, Oliver, 58, 61
Cromwell, Thomas, 20, 21, 23, 28, 29, 30

Davies, Edward (Celtic Davies), 116, 117,
  119-20
Davies, Howell, 73, 74
Davies, Owen, 94
Davies, Pryce, 67, 68
Davies, Richard, 40
Defynnog, 13, 119
Description of Wales, 6, 8
Dickens, Charles, 129
Dinas, 16
Drury Lane, 106, 107-8, 110, 137
Dygoedydd, 69, 75

Edward I, king, 13
Edward III, king, 13
Edward IV, king, 43
Edward VI, king, 21, 30, 31, 34
Einion Sais, 13, 14, 15
Elizabeth I, queen, 34, 35, 41, 46-7, 49
  52, 53, 54

Erasmus, Desiderius, 25
Evans, Theophilus, 74, 115, 123
Expugnatio Hibernica, 5

Fisher, John, 22
Fitzgerald, David, 1, 2, 3
Flemings, 3
Freemasonry, 121-2

Gam, Dafydd, xiv, 13-19, 20
Gam, Gwladus, 18
Games, Hoo, 18
Garrick, David, 106, 107-8
Geoffrey of Henlaw, 10
Geoffrey of Monmouth, 31
George V, king, 145
Gerald de Barri, 10
Gerald de Windsor, 1
Gerster, Etelka, 133-4
Giraldus Cambrensis (Gerald the Welshman), xiv, xv, 1-12
Glanvill, Ranulph, 8
Glyndŵr, Owain, 10, 14, 15, 16
Godley, Eleanor, 41, 46, 47-8, 49, 50, 51
Godley, Henry, 41
Griffith, David, 88, 115-6
Griffith, Madam Sidney, 77-8
Gwynn, Marmaduke, 73, 86

Hales, John, 45, 46
Harris, Howell, xiv, xv, 65-85
Harris, Joseph, 67, 80, 81
Harris, Thomas, 67
Havard, Thomas, 32
Haverfordwest, 72
Henri, Marquis de Caux, 131, 139
Henry I, king, 9
Henry II, king, 3, 4, 5, 8
Henry IV, king, 14-15, 18
Henry V, king, 17, 18
Henry VII, Henry Tudor, king, 56
Henry VIII, king, 16, 20, 21, 22, 28, 29, 31, 34, 120
Hereford, 2, 6, 8, 20, 21, 23, 24, 30, 32, 60, 61, 82, 101
Hiraethog, Griffith, 24
Hodgkins, John, 45-6
Huet, Thomas, 40
Hughes, John, 76, 94
Hywel ap Dafydd, 20
Hywel, lord of Miskin, 13

Innocent III, pope, 9
Ireland, 4, 5, 8, 10, 86, 90, 92, 93, 110
Itinerarium Kambriae, 5-8

James VI (of Scotland), king, 46-7
John of Agnani, 8
John of Leyden, 61
John, prince and king, 5, 8, 10
Jones, Griffith (of Llanddowror), 67, 68-9, 74
Jones, Hugh, 115, 117
Jones, Jenkin (of Llanddeti), xiv, 56-64
Jones, John, 57
Jones, Theophilus, xiv, xv, 13, 115-124
Jones, Thomas (Twm Siôn Cati), 21
Jordan, 3

Kemble, Fanny, 113
Kemble, Roger, 100-1, 102, 103
King, Tom, 106
Knightley, Sir Richard, 43, 45, 46
Knipperdollinck, Bernard, 61, 64*n*

Lawrence, Thomas, 109
Lee, Edward Dunn, 40, 41
Leland, John, 16
Lewis, Sir William, 57
Lincoln, 8, 9, 10
Llanddeti, 57, 59, 60, 63
Llanddew, xv, 3, 5, 14
Llanddowror, 67, 69
Llandovery, 13, 69, 117
Llandrindod, 101
Llanfaes, 6, 115
Llangamarch, 35, 115, 123
Llangorse, 6, 67
Llanidloes, 78
Llanspyddid, 74
Llantrisant, 78
Llanwrtyd, 73, 74
Llwyd, Humphrey, 31
Llwyn-llwyd, 67
Llywel, 13, 14, 115
Llywelyn ap Hywel Fychan, 13, 14, 15
Llywelyn ap Iorwerth, 9-10
Loxdale, Anne, 94
Ludlow, 29, 30, 42
Luther, Martin, 38, 83 (and *n*)

Machynlleth, 15
Madog, Hywel, 20
Madrid, xv, 127
Manorbier, 1, 10

Mansell, Sir Anthony, 57
Mansell, Bussy, 57-8
Mapleson, James H., 133, 134
Marches, Council in the, 29, 42
Martin Marprelate, 42
Mary I, queen, 30, 31, 34
Mary of Bohun, 15
Memorial schools, 98
Miles, John, 60
More, Sir Thomas, 22
Morgan, Sir Charles, 119
Morgan, John, 61, 63
Morgan, Morgan, 125
Morgan, William (translator of the Bible),
    28, 41, 42

Morgannwg, Lewis, 24
Mortimer, Edmund, 16
Moses, Evan, 78, 82

National Eisteddfod, 135-6
Neath, 22-3, 59, 76, 125, 145
Nest, 1
New Radnor, 6, 8
Newton, 18
Nicolini, Ernesto, 125, 130-1, 132, 134,
    135, 137, 138-9

Odile, 140, 142
Owen, George (of Henllys), 54
Owain Lawgoch, 14
Oxford (university), 5, 20, 24, 37, 38, 57,
    58, 67, 68, 88

Paddington, church, 114
Paris, university of, 1, 2, 4, 8
Patti, Adelina, xiv, xv, 125-46
Patti, Salvatore, 127, 128, 130
Penpont, 13
Penry, John, xiv, 34-55, 121
Penry, Meredith, 35
Penwyllt, 136
Peter of Lee, 3, 4, 9
Peyton, William, 14
Pietists, 66
Poitiers, battle of, 13
Poultry Compter, 48-52
Powell, Charles, 80
Powell, Howell, 67
Powell, Susannah, 67
Powell, Vavasor, 58
Price, Gregory, 20, 21, 24
Price, Dame Johan, 20, 21

Price, Sir John, xiv, xv, 20-33
Price, Mary, 117
Price, Rice, 117, 121
Price, Richard, 20, 21, 24, 31
Price, Thomas (Carnhuanawc), 120-1
    (and *n*)
Pritchard, Charles, 83
Puckering, Sir John, 50
Pwll Melyn, battle of, 15

Rhys ap Gruffydd (The Lord Rhys), 4-5
Rhys ap Gwilym, 20
Rhys ap Tewdwr, 1
Richard I, prince and king, 5, 8, 9
Richard III, king, 56
Richard Fawr, 14
Richard Fitztancred, 3
Rothschild, Alfred, 143
Rowland, Daniel, 70, 75, 77, 78
Royal Albert Hall, 135, 139, 140, 145
Rhuthun, 15, 36, 94

Salesbury, William, 40
Scotland, 46, 47, 48, 51, 52, 92, 111,
    112
Selina, Countess of Huntingdon, 76, 80, 81
Seymour, Jane, 21
Sharpe, Henry, 44, 46
Siddons, Sarah, xv, 99-114, 145
Siddons, William, 103-5, 106, 107, 109-10
Slwch, 6, 14
Smith, Penelope Goulding, 94
South Petherton, 89
St David's, 6, 115, 117
St Eluned, 6
St Guthlac, 30
St John the Evangelist, 23, 24, 25, 30,
    96, 139
St Mary's, 92-3, 101, 115
St Michael's, 139
S.P.C.K., 66
St Thomas a Watering, 53
Strakosch, Maurice, 127*n*, 129, 130
Swansea, 72, 125-6, 132, 137, 145

Talgarth, 67, 68, 73, 74, 83
Tenby, 1, 2
Theatre Royal, 103
Thirty-nine Articles, 35
Thomas, Hugh, 13, 15, 23, 118
Thomas, Leyshon, 22-3
Thomas, Sir William ap, 18
Thomas, William, 61

Thornley, Edwin, 98
Throckmorton, Job, 40, 41
Topographia Hibernica, 5
Trefeca, 78-80, 82, 83
Trefeca-fach, 67
Trefeca-fawr, 67
Trefeca-isaf, 80
Triers, 59-60

Upper Baker Street, 114

Vaughan, Henry, 121
Vaughan, Thomas, 23, 24
Vergil, Polydore, 31
Victoria, queen, 129, 137
Vivian, Graham, 125
Vivian, Sir Hussey (Lord Swansea), 125

Waldegrave, Robert, 41-3, 44, 45, 46
Walter, Hubert, 8, 9, 10
Walton, Richard, 45
Ward, John, 99-100
Ward, Sarah, 100-1, 103, 105
Watford, 76
Watkins, Henry, 57

Watkins, Penoyre, 116
Watkins, William, 57
Wesley, Charles, 76, 78, 86
Wesley, John, 67, 75, 76, 79-80, 86, 89, 90-1, 92, 94
Whitefield, George, 69 (and *n*), 75, 76-7, 80
Whitgift, John, 40, 41, 45, 46
Wigston, Roger, 45, 46
William IV, king, 92
William de Barri, 1
William de Capella, 10
William, Thomas, 78
Williams, Anne, 77 (and *n*), 78, 83, 84
Williams, Edward (Iolo Morganwg), 120
Williams, John, 77
Williams, Richard, 20
Williams, William (Pantycelyn), 73-4
Williamson, John, 20
Wyatt, T.H., 125

Yny Lhyvyr Hwnn, 25, 27
Ystradgynlais, 132
Y Wernos, 68